What to Expect When She's Expecting

An Honest Guide to Supporting the New Mom in Your Life

Amy Perry

ISBN-13: 978-0-6488872-0-1

Dedicated to Ashley.

CONTENTS

PART TWO

THE FIRST WEEKS AFTER THE BABY IS

BORN

PART THREE

THE FIRST YEAR

What to Expect When She's Expecting

AUTHOR'S NOTE

This book is my own perspective and understanding of pregnancy and becoming a new mother. I'm not a doctor or a specialist or a midwife. I'm just a typical Millennial in the 2020s, who took a huge interest in delving deeper into others' stories and research after experiencing firsthand how much is missing when it comes to understanding how best to support a new mother today. Generally, the chapters are organized in a way that take you from a woman's pregnancy to the first weeks after giving birth, and finally the first year of the child's life. In each chapter there are general tips for everybody involved in the new mother's life plus some tailored advice for a husband or partner, grandmother, sibling, in-law, or friend, with or without children themselves.

To make the book easier to read without cumbersome repetition of terminology, I refer to the woman's partner as "husband" and use the masculine pronoun for this role but the information is relevant for partners whether married or not, male or female.

Others' stories throughout the book are used with consent from friends who generously shared the details, and sometimes horror stories, of their experiences. Names have been changed for privacy.

INTRODUCTION

What kind of alternate universe is this? I went to the best school in my state, graduating with a triple major from university. In terms of what society views as having a "successful" life, I was director of a medium-sized company, a mentor for other women coming up the ranks, in decent physical shape, in touch with my spirituality, yada, yada, yada.

I was a happy person who had her shit together. Yes, even during pregnancy. I was sure that I knew what I was doing even though it was my first time pregnant. I read books, I researched; I decided to take the easygoing approach and not let anything phase me. Yet here I was, once again, listening to somebody yammer on to me about what they thought I should be doing—in this particular case, aqua fitness for pregnant women. Because, apparently, I didn't have other things to do with my time—what with working, housework, remodeling a new house, as well as preparing for a baby's arrival.

So goes the story of many mothers-to-be and new moms. One can be calm and collected about the idea of taking this journey of pregnancy to motherhood, only to be bombarded with incessant thrashings of "you should," "you must," and "make sure you" about *every tiny thing* from everyone. We're treated like simpletons without a means of forming a decision on our own just because we're pregnant, or with a new baby. It's an experience that too many competent women today are unfortunately battling through.

There is no doubt that pregnancy, and taking care of a newborn, can be a tremendously tiring and demanding time in a woman's life. Often people think that the baby is the main culprit when it comes to a mother's stress. But for many new mothers, this is not the case. In fact, it's the people surrounding us whom (likely unknowingly) cause much more anxiety and stress to the mother than the baby itself.

The words "likely unknowingly" prompted me to write this guide. Nobody intends to stress out their partner, daughter, daughter-in-law, sister, sister-in-law, or friend during this time. But it happens. The fact that you're reading this tells me that you do care for the new mother in your life and that's really wonderful. She'll need and appreciate your support when given in the right way.

Understanding how a pregnant woman or a new mother thinks requires a level of empathy that is almost impossible to reach without having been through the same thing yourself, at a similar point in time, in a similar society and culture (sorry mother-in-law!). You may mean well. You may mean to help. But the things you do or say might be taken in completely the wrong way, leading to hurt feelings, anxiety, stress, irritation, or in worst-case scenarios, broken relationships that could take years to mend. This is a terrible way for a woman to go through pregnancy and surely not the intention of most people who care about her. And after the baby is born, these hurt feelings don't just subside—they're prone to fester, sometimes even grow, and affect the way and frequency in which the mother (and baby) interacts with you.

To try and shine a light on how to be a great partner or friend during a woman's pregnancy and early years of motherhood, I've broken down the reasoning, aiming to help remove the blinders and allow you to better empathize with the thought patterns and shifting reality of the typical new mother or mother-to-be during pregnancy, up to labor and the first few weeks to a year of motherhood. And if you're a loving husband or partner who really just wants to know how best to support your wife or partner during this period, then fantastic. I have loaded the book with tons of tips especially for you.

I truly hope that you will find this guide insightful and helpful in creating a wonderful experience for the expectant mother in your life. It's the book I wish was written when others around me were having children before I had my own. It's the content I will revisit if I myself should one day become a grandmother.

PART ONE

DURING THE PREGNANCY

THE FIRST PREGNANCY

There are many factors in play during a woman's pregnancy. Before showing any physical symptoms, some women are taken hostage by their hormones, bringing their (often blindsided) partners and loved ones along with them on an emotional rollercoaster. Many want to be coddled and taken care of (I mean, we *are* creating life here). Other women feel very energized. And some feel little or no difference to their emotions or energy levels at all. Every pregnancy is different, but amongst all their differences, there are some commonalities, particularly for a relatively informed woman going through pregnancy for the first time.

Neither Unsolicited Advice nor Judgment Is Welcome

With so much conflicting information out there with regards to all things baby, it's not easy for a woman going through pregnancy—especially for the first time—to just sit back and take it easy. It really doesn't help when people start offering advice or casting judgment on what she should or should not be doing.

A first pregnancy is just the beginning of the parenthood journey, and a newly expectant mother is not yet attuned to drowning out all the advice or opinions of others—especially if she's a bit of a people pleaser or too nice to risk being impolite. The truth is that many people see a baby bump as an open invitation to begin giving unsolicited advice and there is no prenatal class that teaches a woman how to Zen out during *that* onslaught. Getting good at this necessary skill can take a while. But not gaining this skill at all can lead to months of inner torment, trying to process the opinions of others, which will more than likely always be conflicting.

We all catch ourselves doing it, if not just to fill an uncomfortable silence. But some people give unsolicited advice more often than others and with more insistence. And *that* is what can be most frustrating to a pregnant woman, because insistence implies that you're judging their current actions.

Physical Changes Can Really Suck

The first trimester is difficult because other people usually cannot see the physical changes happening in the woman's body. But there is so much going on hormonally that the expectant mom may feel extremely tired but also unable to turn down social interactions due to various reasons (e.g., an important family event). In many cases, couples choose not to reveal that they're pregnant until after the first trimester so it can also be tricky (not to mention, stressful) for them to come up with an excuse not to attend or RSVP firmly without it seeming impolite.

If you do know that a woman is pregnant, don't blame her for often needing to rest or seeming glassy-eyed mid-conversation. Be happy that she's out at all. Pregnancy tiredness isn't mild; it's often more like the kind of exhaustion after a full day of heavy labor.

There are many versions of "morning sickness" that vary from woman to woman. Some experience no feelings of nausea at all; others have all the symptoms and are basically bedridden for the first three months. And then there are those who feel it horribly throughout the entire nine months. It's no joke and no fun for anybody. Who knows why it's called "morning" sickness, because in some cases it's headaches and nausea or vomiting the entire day *and night*.

It's a nightmare.

Later, once a woman reaches the third trimester, the silver lining (if I may start there) is that people can now see that she is pregnant as opposed to just packing on the pounds. The dark cloud however, is that physical changes like the obvious weight gain, bloating, and swollen ankles, feet, and fingers that feel like they're about to explode, must be personally experienced before one can begin to imagine or understand. It's a time when some women can no longer control their farts. Others need to pee seemingly every two seconds. Some are constipated all the time. And some unlucky ones suffer from it all.

Don't be offended if the usually happy-go-lucky mom-to-be can no longer commit to meeting up for lunch two weeks out.

Aside from the very real matters regarding the physical aspect of being pregnant, there are so many matters related to pregnancy that can cause anxiety too. A body that is changing so quickly can lead to mild depression in some women. Many worry about the financial impact of having a baby, as well as the loss of freedom or "me time" that raising a child will mean. For a *first-time* mother, mixed in with a bit of fear of the unknown, all of these feelings are often heightened even further.

Becoming Protective

A common phenomenon is that pregnant women become very protective of their unborn child. They will do everything they are told by the doctors *plus* obsessively read up on everything about pregnancy, a baby's first year, and all the way up to raising good children. We're biologically ingrained to protect our young even before they are born. Of course, there are the moments when, despite knowing that caffeine during pregnancy is suboptimal, a woman may be unable to carry on without her daily caffé latte. But more often than not, she's passing on that glass of wine, taking those prenatal vitamins, and avoiding activities that are generally not recommended for women in their first, second, or third trimester.

QUICK QUIZ

So you've decided to throw your friend a baby shower after her first trimester. There's champagne for the guests, but when offered a glass, the guest of honor says she doesn't want to drink. What do you do?

A. Tell her in front of other friends that one drink is fine, to not worry about it, and live a little!

B. Insist that one drink is not going to harm her baby, and force a glass of bubbly into her hand. Geez!

C. Respect her choice. But insist that one drink is fine, backing it up with research you've conducted online that proves your point.

D. Respect her choice and offer her a glass of sparkling cider or seltzer instead.

You may be surprised that anything but answer (D) is not what any expectant mother wants to hear. A lot of people think a pregnant woman wants to be given "allowances," and they are more than happy to be that "voice of reason" to give her the go-ahead, when actually the natural thing a lot of pregnant women want to do, especially for the first child, is everything by the book. Respecting that, even *encouraging it,* is the best thing you can do to show your support.

If you answered (C), you're respecting her choice, *but* to a pregnant woman, your insistence reads like this: "You're being overly precious/cautious. My research and judgment are better than yours. Fine. Don't have a drink, you prude."

Always Err on the Safe Side

When going out with friends to dinner, don't be the person who says, "One piece of salami is fine for the baby. I'm sure toxoplasmosis is only after *too much* salami." Or "That meat is just a little bit rare; it's fine, don't worry." Apart from being factually incorrect, it's always better to err on the cautionary side because it shows a respect for the mother-to-be and the unborn child. Toxoplasmosis can have very serious consequences for an unborn baby, and listeriosis can easily cause miscarriage in the first trimester. *That* is exactly how serious these illnesses can be and why pregnant women are given the information on what they need to avoid.

Sure, you may have indulged in rare meats and smoked salmon while *you* were pregnant, but people's bodies don't all react the same and food quality is not always consistent. If you have never suffered a miscarriage, you can't imagine the sense of guilt, grief, and loss someone who has goes through. Part of it is questioning everything that they did or consumed that *might have* been the cause of it.

Furthermore, think about it this way. If the mother has made the decision to avoid foods that she would normally find desirable, isn't it a bit of an inconsiderate move to try and break down her willpower? Would you encourage a person on a diet to eat a slice of chocolate cake? A gluten intolerant person to have just one bite of bread because it's so fresh and totally worth it? Of course you wouldn't, because it's a plain disregard for their decision and practice of willpower. And with pregnancy, the potential stakes are so much higher.

The ONLY person allowed to make the call on anything except going by the book is the pregnant woman herself. Given the information hurled at her from everywhere and her actual physician, she can come to her own conclusion on what leniency she will give herself and her unborn child.[1]

A woman expecting her second/third/fourth/fifth child may be a little more lenient with herself during pregnancy. Again, that's really her call. If you see her having a glass of wine at dinner, a cup of coffee, or a piece of sashimi, don't go running up to reprimand her. If she's smoking like a chimney or off her face drunk, then modern science has proven that that is just dangerous and stupid, so a bunch of questioning, dirty, judgy looks may be in order. But leave the intervention to her husband or her direct family.

---

1 Remember I am talking about a relatively educated pregnant woman here. If you're dealing with an uneducated person, alcoholic, drug abuser, somebody who is not in their right mind, or one who is exclusively taking medical advice from an unlicensed practitioner like a faith healer, then you need to seek professional help or advice immediately.

WHAT YOU CAN DO THAT WOULD BE APPRECIATED

Cooking

This is a great one. If you don't cook, bringing over store-bought or restaurant food is usually super appreciated and helpful, especially if there are picky eaters in the family or if the expectant mom herself is picky. Just keep in mind that there are a few things that pregnant women often are advised to avoid, including raw/cured meats (think prosciutto), raw fish, shellfish, and sodas or other things with caffeine in them. Veggie salads (even those pre-packaged) need to be washed in baking soda. If she has food cravings that you're aware of, bring them along!

Good company with good food is almost always welcome—especially when pregnant.

Cleaning

Depending on which stage and state the mother-to-be is in, arranging to have someone clean the house is a very nice gesture. Certainly not all women would take you up on this offer, as it is often quite a large gesture, but if you're the husband and you generally don't do the cleaning, outsourcing this task at least once a week could be very helpful, especially as most pregnant women don't want to be exposed to the odors and chemicals in cleaning agents.

Cleaning up is quite another thing. Simple things like loading the dishwasher for a heavily pregnant woman can become strenuous on the back and knees, not to mention uncomfortable on the stomach. Offer to do it, even if you're not at your own house, and then insist.

Massages

I've never heard of a woman complaining about receiving a gift card to the nearest spa offering massages for pregnant women. A lot of places offer massages designed specifically for women in their second and third trimester. This is a welcome way to relax and just be pampered. The main tip here is to not book a massage on a specific date unless you're absolutely sure she will be available and feeling well to go. This is why a gift card works so well. Leave the flexibility to her or you'll be inadvertently gifting potential stress.

Giving Space and No Random Visits

How exciting! Someone's pregnant and they're on leave from work, so they're at home all day doing nothing but waiting for you to pop by, right? Maybe. But it's always safer to call ahead, just in case they have other plans—like sleeping all day. If so, don't take offence. It's not you, it's not them; it's pregnancy. Sometimes pregnancy can really take it out of you. That being said, a lot of women have virtually no symptoms of being pregnant and would really appreciate you visiting. Gauge the situation and go from there. Usually a polite refusal of your visit should suffice to indicate for you not to insist. As long as you know the expectant mother isn't spiraling into depression, and therefore avoiding all outside contact, give her space and wait until she is ready to be social again.

THINGS THAT YOU SHOULD AVOID AT ALL COSTS

Besides being a pregnancy police officer in general, there are some actions that you should never take in order not to damage your relationship with the pregnant woman and cause unnecessary ill will or stress.

Thinking It's More about the Father Than the Mother

There are many times during a pregnancy when, as a third person watching in, you may feel more sympathetic toward the father than the mother. For example, the father is now working longer hours because he is worried about financially supporting his wife and their growing family. Or the father is now taking more time off work to care for his wife with hyperemesis gravidarum (or some version of morning sickness). Or the father is feeling emotionally unable to cope with the anxiety of having a child. You might catch the couple at a moment where the soon-to-be mother is berating the father for not reading a book or two about what to expect when having a child (give him a copy of this!), or for ordering Indian take-out, forgetting that the she has developed a hyper-sensitivity to smells. And now there is tension and stress all around.

As a friend or relative, always keep in mind one thing. If his wife is usually a levelheaded, decent person, everything the father is feeling during this time is most likely *worse* for her. Think about it. She has to deal with whatever issues are going on with her body, her emotional and mental state during all these changes, *plus* her husband, who is now having a bit of a breakdown and likely causing her further stress.

I N HER FINAL TRIMESTER, Sarah gained 23 kg, and was suffering from nausea, bloatedness, and difficulty walking. On top of that, her husband, Rob, was stressing over renovating and moving into a new home before the arrival of the baby. To take matters into her own hands regarding preparations for the baby, she ordered most of the baby's nursery online. Rob, upon finding out, asked her to cancel the order, as he believed he could find better prices elsewhere. For a week he dragged her to shop after shop. In the end, they were unsuccessful.

On a weekend that Rob was away, his sister Flora insisted to Sarah over lunch that they must continue this search together, to surprise Rob, whom she had noted was stressed. When Sarah politely declined her offer, Flora reiterated how stressed her brother was until Sarah felt obligated to go. "I was exhausted by this stage in the pregnancy," Sarah recalled. "I was also pissed off at my husband for needlessly prolonging a process on the endless list of tasks we had to do before the arrival of the baby!"

Flora didn't understand what it was like to be in Sarah's shoes. Her concern was completely focused on

Rob. She didn't realize she had only one side of the situation—his. Flora wasn't being a hero for recognizing and labeling Rob's "stress." She was thinking from one perspective only and totally overstepped her boundaries.

Don't make a similar mistake. It's almost always more difficult for the mother than the father, so if you want to help, help in meaningful ways that can actually alleviate the stress of *both* parents-to-be, not just move the task from the father to the mother. If they really wanted to, they could make that arrangement themselves.

Deciding Which Hospital to Go To Give Birth

It's a very personal choice for a mother which hospital she would prefer to deliver the baby in or whether she prefers to have a homebirth and what her birthing plan is. The factors she may consider include whether the hospital has a neonatal intensive care unit (NICU), the policy on epidurals, the capacity of the hospital, the hospital's rate of complications during childbirth, the number of births carried out at the hospital, the after-birth care facilities for the mother and the baby, the visiting policy, or very simply the name of the city that will be on the baby's birth certificate and ID card.

If you happen to be more informed about the hospitals in the area because you work at one, it's almost always helpful to share your information, keeping in mind that not everyone will place the same importance on factors which you may find integral. For example, if the mother feels safer being at a hospital with a NICU, don't try to make light of the issue and say something like, "Women have been giving birth for thousands of years, even in caves. You don't need a NICU if some maternity wards are in hospitals without them!"

Yes, women have been giving birth for many years without the type of care available today, but the neonatal mortality rate (number of babies that die within their first month after birth) in some OECD countries such as Italy has dropped from 24.7 to 2 per 1000 live births from 1960 to 2018 (twelve-fold!)[2] And infant mortality rates (the number of babies who die within their first year after birth) dropped from 60.41 to 2.3 per 1000 births since 1950. That's thirty-fold! Not only babies but mothers used to suffer far more complications than they do today during labor

---

[2] The World Bank Group, *Estimates Developed by the UN Inter-agency Group for Child Mortality Estimation (UNICEF, WHO, World Bank, UN DESA Population Division) at childmortality.org.* [online] Published 2019, Accessed October 2019.

and after, so it's not silly for a mother to be pedantic about going to a hospital with better facilities for the possibility that a complication could arise. You sure wouldn't want to be the one that made light of the situation, only to have a complication occur during her labor.

If it's the other way around, and the mother wants to have a homebirth, that's also totally *her* choice. If you have your concerns for her health or that of her child, you can have an open conversation as to what her plan is. Ask questions but stay open to actually *listening* to her replies. Chances are she already had the same concerns, yet came to a conclusion. At the end of the day, keep in mind that unless mandated by her OBGYN, the decision on which hospital to go to is completely her own.

Whether or Not to Get Vaccinated

During pregnancy there are a lot of decisions that a mother-to-be must make together with her husband. In countries where it's not yet mandatory, one is the decision to get vaccinated during pregnancy, so that the baby has antibodies and is somewhat protected against whooping cough/pertussis.

Any pregnant woman having done her research wants to protect her child as much as possible. The theory behind vaccinations is that when you vaccinate your child, it helps to completely eradicate some diseases in society. But this only works when the majority of children are vaccinated. Why can't *this* baby be one among those that aren't vaccinated? Because in reality, there are already those who can't, including those who are simply too young to be vaccinated. When this particular baby is born, for some time he or she will be one of those who are "too young to be vaccinated." So getting vaccinated is not only proactive, but helps keep those who can't (and who are often most susceptible to complications) safe from these life-threatening diseases too.

DURING ANNA'S PREGNANCY in Italy, she was told "whooping cough doesn't exist here" or "it was already eradicated here in our country." With so many travelers around the world, that is simply not a valid statement. Two weeks after her insistence on getting the whooping cough vaccination while pregnant and being met with these types of dismissive responses, not one but two babies died of whooping cough at the hospital she was to give birth in. A year later, making this vaccination obligatory for pregnant women made it into Italian parliamentary debate and getting it became "strongly advised" amongst the best hospitals in Italy.

The decision to vaccinate during pregnancy is always the mother's decision where it's not obligatory. At best, it's a decision to be made between the mother and father only. After all, she will have the vaccination and it is her body and her baby.

Among some groups of people there is a strong belief that vaccinations should be avoided. The rationale is often based on a belief that vaccinations are a moneymaking ploy devised by pharmaceutical companies. Or that vaccinations cause autism (a theory that was debunked with the doctor claiming this being stripped of his license to practice). I get it. When there is a precious newborn or to-be-born baby, there is the feeling of nature-created 'perfection'. Why mess with something that isn't broken? We need only look at the willingness to spend on natural and organic options from baby food to diapers to see that we all think this way to some degree.

But we do need to keep in mind that for better or worse, the world has changed. Back in the 'simpler' days, pre-vaccination (aka the 1900s), the average lifespan in the United States of America was 47.3 years.[3] Nowadays, that's about the age we have our

---

[3] Rappuoli, R., Pizza, M., Del Giudice, G., & De Gregorio, E. (2014). Vaccines, new opportunities for a new society. *Proceedings of the National Academy of Sciences of the United States of America, 111*(34), 12288–12293.

midlife crises. There are very strong links to an increase in life expectancy and the introduction of vaccines that calling it a 'coincidence' is just not a valid argument. If the expectant mother in your life happens to be against being vaccinated, there are many good articles[4] and research papers on the subject that you could point her to so that she can be better informed before making a decision. As research papers are never as sexy as articles in glossy yet reputable publications, it might be easier to lead her to one of those.

I heard a case of overbearing relatives who literally stood by the phone when the mother was trying to book her vaccination, giving her looks of disapproval and trying to convince the baby's father not to let her make the appointment. Apart from taking a scientifically and logically incorrect stance, this is completely socially incorrect behavior on all levels. If the relatives in this case didn't even try to open up the subject to an exchange of ideas with the mother (where their points may have been successfully proven

---

[4] Here is an article with graphs you might like to refer to. Conniff, R. (16 August, 2019). The World Before Vaccines is a World We Can't Afford to Forget. *National Geographic Society,* Accessed on 2 June 2020.
[https://www.nationalgeographic.com/culture/2019/08/cannot-forget-world-before-vaccines/]

invalid), then they definitely shouldn't have swept in at the last moment to insist upon their beliefs. In such a situation, it doesn't matter if you are the expectant mother's sibling, parent, in-law or how close you think you are to the family. It doesn't matter if you're to be the baby's godmother or godfather. It's simply not your place.

This is particularly sensitive because you are imposing your opinion on what is strictly the mother's physical body and what you think she can or cannot do with it. The feeling of being out of control of the decisions for your own body can lead to depression or a very deep feeling of resentment toward you for thinking that you have *any* right to this decision. Relationships often take years to heal after these types of boundaries are not respected. Tread very lightly here. In fact, don't tread at all.

Insisting the Expectant Mother Attend Social Events

If you've never been heavily pregnant, don't expect a woman in her last trimester to do physically strenuous activities. The definition of "physically strenuous" can run the whole gamut from grocery shopping to painting the nursery. That being said, this depends a lot on the pregnancy. Some (I want to say 'very few' as to not accidentally raise your expectations) women feel energized during pregnancy, all the way up to labor. But some really don't.

A woman once told me the story of her pregnancy, where her sister-in-law made insistent and indignant comments, such as "You can't turn down the invitation to that lunch!" for a luncheon that was scheduled on her baby's due date! Whenever she would want to rest instead of going out, her sister-in-law would remind her, "My mom was doing the laundry right up until her water broke." Needless to say, she herself had never been pregnant. Otherwise she'd be able to understand that not all pregnancies are the same. Comparisons to a pregnancy that is not your own reads like judgment.

Don't accidentally be that person. After the baby arrives, there are plenty of times without your help that a mother will feel inadequate. It doesn't need to start before. By all means, invite your pregnant friends to soirées. You can even let them know what they're missing out on if they don't go. But try to be respectful of the fact that they might simply be too tired, too uncomfortable, or too busy to attend.

Making Hurtful Comments Like "You Don't Strike Me as the Maternal Type"

You may be totally convinced that the mother-to-be does not seem to be mother material. Perhaps for your liking, she's too career-driven, cold as a person, or far too selfish to be maternal. However, even if you may already be a mother yourself, it's not your place to judge. On top of that it's not a nice thing to hear— even if you don't intend for any comment to be hurtful.

Women who are pregnant need to hear that they will be fine when the baby arrives. No matter what, they're going to be able to make it work. They will arrange themselves and their lives to become decent mothers. Even if she has never seemed to be at ease around other kids before, there's no need to jump to conclusions and point these out to her. There are all types of mothers, all doing a fine job raising children. Don't accidentally project your stereotype of what a mother "should" be onto somebody else. It is insensitive. Besides that, it's a little late. It's like telling a surgeon just as she steps into the operating theater, "You don't strike me as the type that could save somebody's life."

Insisting on Your "Tried and True" Pregnancy Tips

There are tips amongst the older generation, such as "Have a glass of red wine every day to give you more energy during pregnancy," that may not go down quite so well with those who have grown up in the information age.

You don't always know the backstory to a person's pregnancy. Perhaps they have been trying to get pregnant for years. Maybe they have been through excruciating rounds of IVF. Or they have suffered miscarriages. You simply *don't know* because often this information is not shared as openly as a pregnancy past twelve weeks. Don't insist on anything other than going by the book. And don't take offence when your advice is not taken, although it worked for you. A pregnant woman may well be pedantic because she sees the importance of creating the vital organs and anatomy of this baby that need to endure not only the entire pregnancy, but the child's lifetime. Any risks associated with veering off the doctors' advised path is simply not worth it to her.

Treating the Pregnant Person like an Invalid

If a woman goes through a particularly difficult first trimester, it can be difficult for you to switch back to the mindset that she is back to her usual self—even if she's feeling fine in her second and third—and no longer needs to be treated like a delicate flower. In trying to be helpful in those first months, you may accidentally treat her situation as a condition and overcompensate in areas where she actually doesn't need any help. For example, her mental state may still be relatively intact to make decisions on certain things, such as which physician to see, and this is invariably her decision. As a relative or a friend, you don't need to make these decisions for her. In fact, doing so may be seen as overstepping your boundaries.

If she is back to her usual self and wants to exercise or wishes to work up to the delivery date, then so be it. There is no need to offer pity or react in shock. Think about it, does being the subject of a pity party ever feel good? In most cases, it often makes us feel worse. It's always better to respect her wishes. If there were any real concerns, her doctor would have advised her already.

Being Negative or Enabling and Encouraging Negativity

There is a lot of research that shows stress hormones released during pregnancy can affect the unborn baby. This is why a pregnant woman is often encouraged to engage in relaxing activities, think positive thoughts, and surround herself with positive energy. To some, a baby being able to "feel" the mother's emotions from the womb may sound very far-fetched, a bit too New Age, or woo-woo. Let's take one step back from "emotions" and talk science and chemicals. At continuously high levels, the stress hormone cortisol is shown to adversely affect the growth of the fetus. Research is also beginning to show that this may affect mood disorders in children as they grow up.

Often pregnant women find themselves becoming very sensitive to negative comments made by others, be them about herself or about anything in general, where she cannot actively distance herself from the negative person.

CLAIRE, A MOTHER OF TWO RECALLS, "When I was pregnant with my first child, my brother's wife would often come over unannounced 'just to chat' and then proceed to complain about *everything*. Sometimes it wasn't even the things she was saying; it was just the whiny, victim-like tone she used to make comments like 'I have to go and buy a present for my friend's birthday but I don't want to,' or 'Oh god, it's raining again today, there's just no end to this, is there?' Ironic, because although there *was* an end to the unfavorable weather, there was no end in sight to her foul attitude. Generally I don't support victim mentality like this. But while pregnant, I was often tempted to just kick her out of my home! I would have to shake off her negative aura after she left every day."

Some pregnant women fall into a mild state of anxiety, or engage in negative thinking, as their bodies begin to change and they feel they are losing control or worry that they are not yet ready to be mothers. This can make them even more susceptible to hopping onto a negativity bandwagon. You can help by listening to her issues, aiding where you can, but trying not to enable the negative thinking or allowing things to blow out of proportion. It's easy to go down that spiral, but in the end, it won't do anyone any favors.

Insisting on Your Birthing Plan

How she would prefer to give birth is one of the most personal choices a woman will make in life. Unless advised by her doctor otherwise, how she gives birth is up to her. Vaginal birth, C-section, epidural, laughing gas or natural birth—these are all decisions that a pregnant woman will make and potentially execute. I say "potentially" because there are plenty of cases where women plan to have an epidural but then arrive too late at the hospital and end up going the natural route. There are also those who plan to go natural and then realize that they want an epidural during contractions. Then, of course, there are those who require emergency C-sections or a vacuum-assisted delivery. So, even if carefully planned, things may not always go as envisioned. This is why it's not only overbearing but actually useless for you to insist on *your* particular birthing plan for a birth that does not involve your own physical body.

And if you haven't given birth before—especially if that reason is because you're a man—you should not be giving *any* advice on a birthing plan. Don't push the benefits of a doula, or having or not having a private midwife, whether to give birth in a water tub, what position to give birth in, and which pain relief methods to use or refuse. Everyone's pain threshold is different and if *they* can't even gauge how they will handle childbirth, it would be far too presumptuous to imagine that you could.

Another thing to be careful of is not to judge someone who wants to give birth with their hair and make-up done, so that they are ready for those inevitable post-delivery photos. Times are different now with social media, accessible cameras, and video. It's completely normal for a woman to want to look as good as possible after just having given birth. Can they wear contact lenses? Yes. Make-up? Sure. Nail polish? Depends. Probably better not to, in case they need to have a C-section, in which case the answer is no.

Husbands, if you'll be in the delivery room, one of your jobs is to take the most flattering photo possible of new mom with baby. Don't stop clicking until you get that shot!

THE UNSPOKEN RULES REGARDING THE DELIVERY

Natural birth or C-section? Epidural or no Epidural? Who can be in the delivery room? It should go without saying that these decisions are strictly up to the expectant mom if they are not mandated by her physician. Not even the husbands get to have a say on these. Really. Under every single circumstance. Sorry dads (or should I say, thank your lucky stars), the delivery is more or less all about the mother. Yes, she may be birthing your child, but if she says no when you ask if your parents or siblings can be there during the delivery, there are no two ways about it. Look on the bright side, at least it's not you that will be going through painful contractions, possibly a multitude of birthing positions, vein-popping pushing all while praying not to poop. But I digress.

Being there during the delivery to "witness" the birth of your future grandchild and live out all those emotions in real time may seem like a great idea to you. Who doesn't love a bit of drama, right? But for many women, unless you're the husband, this is overstepping the boundaries.

It is also overstepping boundaries if you are encouraging the baby's father to be in the delivery room, or *especially* if you are *discouraging* him to be where the expectant mother wants the opposite.

S ARAH WAS EXPECTING her first child and wanted her husband, Rob, to be there. Rob was sitting on the fence because he was worried about having the images of a natural birth imprinted in his mind, but Sarah wanted him there for moral support, not to cut the umbilical cord. Rob's sister, Flora, told him that it wasn't important to be there in the delivery room. She also told Sarah not to pressure Rob because he would be traumatized and it would be too much for him to handle. Rob is a fully functional, grown-ass man. Sarah was livid because it was a discussion between her husband and herself. Flora, not having ever given birth, didn't understand the emotional aspect of the process and would have done better just keeping quiet.

TIPS FOR HUSBANDS

Your sister, with whom you are very close and who has had four children in Hospital A, highly recommends that you and your wife go to the same hospital. Your wife is leaning toward Hospital B, which she wants to check out. You're quite convinced that Hospital A is the better option. What do you do?

A. Reason with your wife as to why Hospital A is better. But take your wife to check out the other hospital anyway.
B. Go with your wife to check out Hospital B.
C. Lay out all the reasons Hospital A is fine and decide that is the hospital in which she will deliver the baby.
D. This is a no-brainer; the decision is already made. Hospital A, of course. Your sister had four perfectly healthy children there!

This is not a trick question. The answer is (B).

Answer (A) is just creating unnecessary stress to your wife. You're going to take her to check out

Hospital B anyway. Do that and let her make the decision on her own, unless she is actively seeking your advice. Answers (C) and (D) are just completely incorrect. It's her body that they will take care of during and after the delivery. Not yours and not your sister's. In any case, she may have different standards or expectations than that of your sister.

**THE BIGGEST TIP**: Always be on your wife's side. ALWAYS. Your relationship with your wife during this time is tremendously important. If it's off, then it could lead to a snowball effect where everything else falls apart.

A first pregnancy may be a time of excitement and joy, but it can often be a time of enormous tension, miscommunication, confusion, and overwhelming pressure for you both. Your wife may be behaving erratically. She may be emotional. She may be physically weak. Her moods and state can be unpredictable and generally quite unpleasant to be around at times.

The first trimester of the first pregnancy can be a time when your wife feels very vulnerable and delicate. This period is usually the riskiest for miscarriage and she knows this. Plus it can be an extremely difficult time for a woman suffering from morning sickness. If you haven't been doing so already, now is the time she will appreciate being coddled and taken care of to some extent. If she's unwell, then you've really got no choice and it could be quite a task. But remember, however bad you think you've got it, more than likely, she's got it worse. Your social life is no longer able to be planned for the foreseeable future, and your sex life is probably dead or minimal too. Don't worry, it will pass. It may take a few months until the end of the first trimester or even the first four months. Worst case scenario, it will take until a couple of weeks after the baby is born, but it will pass.

How Do You Survive This Pregnancy?

Being the partner of somebody who is pregnant for the first time is not always easy. Depending on how the pregnancy is going, you may be dealing with someone whose emotions are highly unpredictable. You yourself may start to feel overwhelmed. This can make even the gentlest of souls start questioning what they have gotten themselves into and why. Many times, all it takes is a change in perspective to give you hope, and staying informed to keep you feeling involved.

Here are a few tips for you on how to get through (and possibly enjoy) these nine months.

Remind Yourself Why You Love This Person Daily

It might help to draft a list of gratitude (and sweet reminders) in your phone just to readily refer to when times are particularly tough. At low points your partner may no longer resemble the person you've described in your list, so it's important that you write down specific memories and moments where you felt lucky to have this person in your life. Pro tip: You want to make your list *before* shit starts hitting the fan because that can happen without a moment's notice.

Gratitude

As cliché as it may sound, putting everything into perspective and feeling grateful that you're able to conceive and go through this in the developed world can help a lot. Pregnancy is only nine months. In the grand scheme of things, this is not very long at all. Even if you had to absorb more than your prior fair share of household duties, massage your wife's feet and fetch every exotic fruit, ice-cream flavor or McDonalds' meal at odd hours for these nine months, it would only be for around 270 days. It's really not much to ask.

Start the Days with Something Nice

A nice gesture like making breakfast for your wife shows that you care and that you appreciate her. It doesn't have to be a full-blown Gordon Ramsay affair. I remember when I was pregnant my husband would fix me a cup of coffee, two pieces of toast with peanut butter and honey, and a cut and peeled kiwi every morning. Not exactly gourmet, but I really appreciated the gesture and it brightened my often difficult mornings, setting me up for the day – even if that meant climbing right back into bed after brushing my teeth. Welcome to a glimpse into the realities of morning sickness.

Keep Yourself Occupied around the House If It Doesn't Stress You Out (And Inadvertently Your Partner)

During your wife's pregnancy, you may sometimes feel a bit useless in that you can't "fix" her bad mood or her aches and pains. What you *can* do is fix up the house for the baby's arrival. Or just fix up the house in general. It keeps your mind busy and you can make use of yourself while staying close to home instead of going out. Sure, you're not making a baby, but putting together some IKEA furniture can offer its own rewarding sense of accomplishment.

Inform Yourself

The changes are happening to her body, but to feel involved in the process, you can inform yourself with information from reputable sources such as NHS or with an easy to follow along app on the phone such as BabyCenter. Ideally, both you and your wife are reading from the same source. If your wife wants to go to prenatal classes where husbands are invited to join, do your best to be in attendance. The delivery is all about your wife, but the days after—taking care of the baby—are about you both as a team.

Always Take Your Wife's Side When Other People Weigh in on Her Pregnancy

Throughout the entire pregnancy, your wife may be hearing everybody weigh in on all sorts of topics, from what exercises she should be doing, what she should or should not be eating, which doctor or hospital she should be going to, and if she should start enrolling her unborn child into a competitive school. On top of this, there will be those who don't believe she might feel unwell and make it known to her that they think she's exploiting her pregnancy to get out of work, housework, or other responsibilities. Your job? To be on her side, always. That's the secret to a happy wife that won't resent you all throughout the pregnancy and after the baby is born.

Communication is Paramount

Having a baby can make or break you as a couple. It's a mammoth responsibility that changes both of your lives, and that's what it's supposed to do. The key is to make sure that this experience strengthens your relationship. How you support each other during the pregnancy sets the tone for how you will parent together. Communication is paramount. As the husband, make sure that you stay appreciative of the fact that your wife is basically putting her life as she knew it before on hold while creating your family. This is a huge commitment and she deserves not to be alone in this.

Spoil Her a Bit—Pregnancy Is Not a Stroll in the Park

Remember that you can't outsource the task of taking care of your wife during this time to a professional, a friend, your mother, or somebody else, unless she can be as forthright and honest with them as she can with you. If she has a close family or a circle of friends upon whom she can call on, they may be able to help you out by taking some of the pressure off you during a tough pregnancy. But other than that, just stick it out. It will be worth it. Show how appreciative you are that she is carrying your child. This doesn't necessarily mean that you need to go out and buy her roses and jewelry *every day*. Both small gestures, like bringing her breakfast, and larger gestures, like going to all the classes and interviewing midwives, doulas, or night nurses, are all good ways to show your appreciation and understanding that it's not easy for her.

THE DELIVERY OF YOUR BABY

As the husband, especially if this is the first child, it is important to show solidarity and a great deal of support during the delivery of the baby. This whole situation is about her, so if she wants you to be in the delivery room with her, you really need to be there. Don't underestimate the importance of this because if you're not there and there isn't so much as a pandemic to stop you from being there, the resentment could run deep. You can't sub in your own mother, a maid or somebody else to be there instead of you. Your wife is delivering your baby, not an Amazon package. This is an important time in her life, and also quite a significant milestone (hello, being born and brought into this world) for your child. A woman is not being dramatic if she asks that you be there and you are not. It doesn't matter if your father was not there when your mother gave birth. Times are different. If you live in the free world, then you need to prepare your schedule around those weeks to really try and be there.

Do the hospital visits prior to the birth with her. A lot of hospitals require that a legal waiver be signed in case she chooses to have an epidural. Some hospitals require that the expectant mom goes in for an examination prior to childbirth. Find out what the situation is and go with her if you can. Find out if you will be able to stay at the hospital on the day that your wife gives birth. If the facilities are available for you to stay (be it another bed or a couch for you to sleep on), then stay. It should go without saying but a lot of men actually are not aware how much their support means to a woman who has just given birth. STAY. Don't go home to "freshen up" or to "take a nap" or "to make a few phone calls." Stay at the hospital with your wife and your newborn child.

Remember the mistake of "thinking it's more about him than it is about her"? This is another scenario in which to keep that in mind.

F RANCESCA RECOUNTED the story of the birth of her first child. "My husband, Giorgio, was there during the delivery. It was a long, painfully drawn out labor. After eight hours in the delivery room, he announced that he was tired, and sweating, and had back pain from sitting in the hospital chair. Aside from having his priorities all wrong, where was his concern for me? Was he not excited to be meeting his firstborn in just a few hours? This was no cakewalk for me! Yet, there he was complaining and almost indignant that I did not acknowledge his pain at the time when I was trying to push a baby out.

"I told him to just go home, have his shower, and enjoy dinner. And he actually *did!* Can you believe it? Even the midwife was shocked. Then after the birth, he didn't stay with me at the hospital, where they wheeled in the baby to stay in the double bed room with me. After a sixteen-hour labor followed by surgery to remove the placenta. There was a bed for Giorgio to stay. When I asked him to remain with me, he said he was tired. He called his mother for validation that he should go home. I heard her say, 'Yes Giorgio, you poor thing; you're tired. You need to go home.' And he did.

"I knew at that moment that my marriage was over. I felt used, and abandoned. It didn't matter that I had just had our child. The bigger 'child' would always be more important and his enabling mother would always validate his behavior. The resentment I felt toward him and to my mother-in-law just grew from there. It was the beginning of the end."

I can't tell you how many women have told me similar stories and how long and deep this resentment runs. There are women who years after still feel that sense of abandonment by their husbands after childbirth. You don't want to make such an easily avoidable mistake. For women, the delivery is usually the most intimidating part of "having children." If your wife asks you to be there, I repeat, *be there*.

For men, the birth is usually seen as the climax of the nine months. Finally, that testing and perhaps grueling phase of pregnancy and your wife's changing hormones is over. Phew! You survived! Now you can go home, have a shower, and relax while your wife's in the hospital recuperating for a couple of days, right? Wrong. Once the baby is born, it's all about getting in there as soon as possible to learn the ropes. Learn your role as a father well.

After giving birth, it's quite unbelievable that you as a couple are given just a day or two's instruction before being able to take this whole other human being who is now reliant on you, home. Make sure you are there for these essential days—particularly if your wife had a long labor, or some complications. But even if she didn't, be there.

Many hospitals will keep the baby in the mother's room. So while she is supposed to be getting rest, she is also perhaps anxious and unsure of what she should be doing with the newborn. Welcome to sleep deprivation. In this sleep-deprived state of recuperation, she is also supposed to be "learning" how to take care of this child from the hospital. If you can be there to learn the routine—simple things like how to diaper, clean the belly button area, dress and swaddle the baby—it would be the least you could do at this stage.

THE PUSH PRESENT

The idea of a "push present" has well and truly arrived, perhaps more so than the *babymoon*. So if you're not on-board, chances are that your wife is and she will be a bit sour if you don't get her a small gift for birthing your child. Push presents are often pieces of jewelry, but there is no hard and fast rule. Anything that might serve as a nice memento of the occasion in the future is usually appreciated.

IN A NUTSHELL

The tips here of being supportive and showing solidarity are not intended to make you feel like a doormat; they will all help in making your wife feel cherished and appreciated. This will strengthen your bond, as many steps in parenthood often do. Throw in a bit of making her feel attractive and you're setting a good tone for things to come. And this will make it easier for her to adopt motherhood without losing a sense of self and who she is to you too.

MOTHERS, SISTERS, AND BROTHERS

THE IMPORTANCE OF CANDOR

If there were ever a time when a girl needs her mother (this includes mother-figures) during her adult life, it would be through pregnancy and the first few weeks, sometimes months, after giving birth. Siblings with a relatively good relationship are usually also a big source of support. Normally if your daughter or sister is pregnant, and you have a healthy relationship, she will tell you exactly what she is feeling, thinking and what she needs for you to do or stop doing. She will appreciate being able to be open and honest about her experience, as this candor is not quite the same with her in-laws.

This doesn't give her the right to use you as a doormat or a punching bag, but know that during this time she may just need somebody to hear her out. You can also be just as honest with her about how pregnancy might be affecting her personality. There are often some effects of hormones that pregnant women themselves cannot see, or otherwise may not attribute to pregnancy. It can take a person with whom we have candor to speak up and tell us that we're being particularly unreasonable or unbearable.

Keep in mind that if she used to work and now she's not working because she is unwell or because she is taking leave, you may hear a lot more from her than usual. The general guide is not to say things that you would not want to hear if you were in her position. Offer advice when asked. Let her vent if need be. Offer a different perspective if she's down about something. Or offer to go and help her out if she is unwell and you are able to. That's what family is for.

DON'T ASSUME "SHE'S GOT THIS"

Mothers, this is your time to step up your game. If you are able to help out, bring food, keep her company if she's alone, or spend time on the phone if she calls. Never assume "she's got this," especially if she tells you that she doesn't! Your anecdotes about how times were so much harder when you were pregnant are not welcome if you're recounting them to try to make her feel inadequate. She will remember this time and it will affect how much exposure she will give you to your future grandchild.

BIANCA WAS PREGNANT with her first child and living in a foreign city, as her husband's work had taken them there. She didn't have a network of friends or family around and her husband was often traveling or putting in long hours at his demanding job. He wouldn't acknowledge the fact that she was going through some pretty big changes and the baby was due soon. When Bianca called her mother to see if she could make it over for the baby's due date, as her husband would not be in town, her mother refused with all kinds of excuses. She had a social event to attend and coolly said, "Don't worry, you'll be fine. You can do this! It's not a big deal. I gave birth without your father around. He was working in a different city at the time too!"

Bianca felt so alone and resented both her mother and her husband. It took her many arguments and a full year thereafter to mend from this feeling of being neglected.

TRICKY SITUATIONS

If your daughter or sister is going through a particularly tricky time, such as bickering with her husband to near-divorce during her pregnancy, offer the best advice you can, keeping in mind that it's also a period of constantly shifting hormones for her. If she has come to the conclusion that divorce is the only option, hear her out and try to gauge whether her reasoning is valid or exaggerated.

One of the key reasons that siblings can offer relatively sound advice is because, traditionally, you grew up together with shared experiences and values. You may have similar views of how you were parented and would more likely be able to understand your sister's fears or anxiety. When you need to pull her out of a rut, you would most likely be forgiven for being somewhat blunt where others would not be. And finally, if you offer humorous relief from a tricky situation or during tougher moments, they would more likely be judged as humorous versus insensitive.

THE IN-LAWS

PARENTS-IN-LAW

When the partner of your son (or perhaps daughter) is expecting their first child, you may not be able to contain your excitement, especially if the baby is going to be your first grandchild. There is almost nothing more exciting than welcoming a new grandchild to the family. You're probably already thinking of the lovely days out with them in the stroller, friends on the street stopping to gush over how cute they are, the sleepovers, the abundant kisses and cuddles.

However, during the pregnancy some things *not to do* include:

- Don't touch the expectant mother's tummy if she has not invited you to! Remember that your comfort level may not match hers. It would be weird, if not unsettling, for somebody to reach over and start rubbing your stomach, right? For some mothers-to-be, this is what the experience can be likened to.
- Don't smoke around the expectant mom.
- Don't share stories of when you were pregnant and handling things so much better than her.

A key point to remember is that regardless of how much control over your son you think you have the right to, that right does not transfer to your daughter-in-law just because she married him. It doesn't matter what kind of family you're from, if you've already set up a trust fund for the baby, or even if you think the mother is incompetent—you just don't have the right to control what she does during pregnancy. This means that during her pregnancy, if you live nearby and are a relatively close family, you can offer support in ways like cooking and setting up the nursery. And in scenarios where your son may not be the greatest partner because he's piling on the stress to his wife, you can help by reining him in, not by supporting his "logic." These are all actions that your daughter-in-law will notice and appreciate.

If you don't live close by, organizing to visit and stay at your son's home during the pregnancy should be avoided. Even if you think you're the most easygoing person on Earth, it's still always a burden on your daughter-in-law.

Err on the Side of Caution

Another important point is to be cautious rather than completely blasé about the pregnancy. If you're not well-informed, either get educated or don't offer an opinion based on "what I remember," because the times have changed. Research into fetal development has grown in leaps and bounds.

The person most likely to be well-advised, who has done recent research, is the mother. There are so many ways to prepare for the arrival of a baby and unless the baby's mother is truly naïve, there's no need for you to add your "you should," "you must," or "it's better if you'" to *anything* baby-related. Just don't do it. Why? Because likely your advice will go in one ear, out the other at best. Or the insistence will turn into something of a grudge against you and could effectively limit your time with the new baby upon its arrival to prevent any more unsolicited advice or opinions.

Times Are Different

Often mothers and fathers-in-law truly mean well and care a great deal about the well-being of their unborn grandchild and loved ones. They just want the best for them. As such, it may be difficult to see your son and his wife try to do everything by the book and sometimes in a manner that is less than ideal for their stress levels. It was never that complicated before, right? Sometimes it seems pregnant women are less resilient than they once were years ago when started a family. They may seem able to endure less and expect more when it comes to being pregnant. However, it should be remembered that times are now different. The stressors and expectations have changed, so just as there is a healthy dose of respect for how you may have gone through pregnancy, there should be the same for how she is doing so.

Give Space

It may be difficult to take a step back, but unless otherwise requested by your pregnant daughter-in-law, taking a step back is the right thing to do in terms of giving advice or insisting on helping. Right now, space and privacy, along with communication, is what's needed between the pregnant couple. Your voice in either one of their ears could potentially become a source of tension, and do more harm than good.

BROTHERS AND SISTERS-IN-LAWS

By now you may have gotten used to your brother's (or sister's) wife being in your life. If you are close with your brother and his wife's a relatively nice person, you may even get along well with their little family. The tricky part is that it doesn't matter whether in your mind your brother is always going to be your little brother, or bigger brother—you actually don't have a say in the way he or his wife choose to prepare for the child during the pregnancy.

The Changing Relationship Between You and Your Brother

A creeping feeling of insecurity can be completely subconscious. Where you once were one of the main influences on your brother's life, a new dynamic exists. In response, you may start "marking your territory." Small actions like casually drinking from his cup over a meal with him and his wife, eating from his plate, or making comments referring to people and things his wife doesn't know. Those are clear indicators that to some degree you feel an "ownership" over your brother that you're not entirely comfortable sharing. A friend of mine's sister-in-law made a big display over a family dinner by throwing the passive-aggressive question out to her brother, "I was thinking about Gemma the other day! God, I miss her! What is she up to now?"

Gemma being an ex-girlfriend that the wife had no idea about until after.

This embarrassing behavior may be difficult to recognize, let alone change but it's something you will have to work on because, especially when the baby is born, you need to live with the fact that your imposing may not be welcome, or else *you* may not be welcome in the child's life.

There are new boundaries when your brother has his own family. They include situations where you give your advice, expecting that it be followed. There are also boundaries regarding your presence. For example, you should not have a key to his home to just pop over whenever you wish. And you shouldn't start planning social events or vacations with your brother—especially if they don't include his wife. Most importantly, it's not your household. Respecting that this pregnancy journey is *theirs,* and doesn't directly involve you, is crucial to your relationship with them.

If you've always had a way in influencing your brother's opinion, this is the time for you to take a step back and realize that your opinion should only be given when asked for. It doesn't matter if you've had a baby before, and you did it this way or that. It doesn't matter if you had vaccinations or not. Or if you went to this hospital or that one. When it comes down to it, during a woman's pregnancy, your opinions are opinions about what somebody else should do with their bodies. So keep them to yourself. Not you and your brother. Yourself.

FRIENDS/RELATIVES WHO HAVE BEEN PREGNANT BEFORE

By far the most supportive group a pregnant woman can have during this time is that of friends who have been through it themselves. And the more recent they have been pregnant, the more relatable and potentially helpful. Don't underestimate how much you can help a woman out during this time if this is you. Because when you speak from firsthand experience, the consolation offered as a woman is going through what seems like never-ending nausea hell, the assurance that it will pass soon, the empathetic anecdote from your own experience, or simply listening and caring, is much more appreciated.

You remember what it was like when you were pregnant—the vulnerability, the discomfort, the fears. You might not be a professional in the field of pregnancy, but what you say holds weight because it comes from *your own* experience. Any comments you make will seem less judgmental *because* they're from your experience, not borrowed experiences from others. If you happen to be a friend or a close relative, it's likely that your values are similar to those of your pregnant friend, so you will naturally be able to empathize with her during her pregnancy.

HAILEY RECALLS, "When I was pregnant in a foreign country, friends who were already mothers with whom I had lost touch contacted me out of the blue to ask how I was doing. I received so much love, so much support from these women. Daily, frequent messaging back and forth, video calls, care packages. They really kept me sane during the hardest days and they made me feel like I could get through it. Some of them had been through worse, all while not being or even seeming condescending."

Always Pay It Forward

Friends who are mothers are just the best. They often reach out with encouragement or advice to friends, even those they now only see on social media struggling with pregnancy. It's a reminder that we as humans are social creatures who became the strongest species because of our capacity to work and support in communities.

A SHORT LIST OF SOME THINGS YOU CAN DO THAT MAY HELP:

- Listen. Nothing beats being heard by someone who has been there before and knows all too well the difficulties of pregnancy.
- Share your own experience with pregnancy or with that particular phase of the pregnancy.
- Encourage and offer hope. A simple line like "It will get better after the first trimester, I promise" can mean so much coming from someone who knows what they're talking about. Some expectant mothers just need to hear from someone who has been through it before, that there is light at the end of the tunnel and they will get through this.
- Offer suggestions or information of what you did when you came across the same issue.
- Respond to her cries for help, whether they are short outbursts over the phone, texts, or posted on social media. And do so as soon as you can.
- Send thoughtful care packages to show that you care.
- Share your resources. If you read a good book, saw a good physician, found some great maternity wear, sharing is caring.

- Pass on any good ideas you may have carried out during your pregnancy (e.g., banking your baby's umbilical blood, taking a photo of the bump each month as a keepsake, etc.).

A NOTE ON THE PREGNANCY AND PARENTING POLICE

This section of the guide is for friends or relatives, not pregnancy or parenting police. Almost nothing is more annoying (okay, enraging) than the pregnancy or parenting police. These are the judgmental fools who think that only the way *they* did pregnancy is acceptable. Sometimes you may find yourself falling into this category and this is when you need to check yourself. It's one thing to share your stories and what you learned from your experience. But it's really another to judge somebody else because they are doing something differently to how you did it.

How do you know if you're being judgmental?

1) If you catch yourself labeling someone as a "good" or "bad" future mother based on one or two things that they do or don't do (e.g., "She's

going to be a terrible mother; she's pregnant and still drinking coffee!")

2) You can't tolerate that someone is not doing something the way you think is best. For example, they are avoiding raw fish while pregnant and so you keep hammering in to them that they can in fact eat raw fish, the risk of listeria food poisoning is for the mother and not the baby. You then conclude that they are being much too protective and precious over the pregnancy.

3) When somebody shares a story with you and you immediately tell them how they should have behaved or what to do from now on, then chances are you're being judgmental. If they haven't told you that anything is wrong, their story is not an invitation to dissect where they went wrong. You telling them how to "fix" the situation can be an indication that you are judging them. For example, your pregnant friend posted a photo on social media of her fetal ultrasound. When you catch up with her you tell her, "Don't be one of *those* moms. Poor kids these days have no privacy whatsoever."

4) If you jump to conclusions and start labeling the mother as "caring too much about her weight" or "being superficial even during

pregnancy" or "letting her inner piggy take advantage of being pregnant" because you think she's eating either too little or too much, gaining too little or too much weight, then you're being judgmental. Her doctor will tell her if she's gaining too much or too little and everyone else need not worry, let alone draw their conclusions as to why.

5) When you can't believe that a future *mother* is wearing *that* outfit while pregnant. If you catch yourself projecting your image of what a mother should be onto somebody else, then you're being judgmental. It would help to remind yourself that there are so many types of mothers in the world and they are raising healthy, well-adapted children.

Being a pregnancy police officer doesn't end with just whether or not you are expressing your concerns directly to the pregnant woman. Casting judgments and telling others, such as the woman's husband or family in a concerned manner does not make one any less annoying, or their advice any more welcome. These are concerns that a pregnant woman would have more than likely already heard and made a decision upon.

FRIENDS OR RELATIVES WITHOUT CHILDREN

Unfortunately there are some women who upon becoming pregnant, begin to think the world and all its inhabitants revolve around them. We all know that woman whose every comment is about how #blessed she feels and how "oh sure," she can go to the cinema with you "because the *baby* will enjoy the sounds from the womb," without so much as mentioning that *she* might also like to be there in your company. You'd be forgiven for rolling your eyes thinking, "yeah alright, nobody asked for your life story". She most likely doesn't even realize she's doing this. If you desperately want children and haven't any yet, chances are that your pregnant friend isn't trying to hurt you; she's just not being thoughtful of others at all. The upside is that you *know* the universe does not in fact revolve around her just because she is now with child, and you can choose not to be around if she is making you feel sad, jealous, invisible, or if she's just become too annoying to handle without a three drink minimum.

For the rest of this section, I'm going to assume that the pregnant friend in your life is one of the bearable ones that you still want to spend time with. At times it can be awkward to listen to all the troubles of pregnancy without having much to add to a conversation. How can you relate when you've never been through pregnancy before? What do you say so that you don't accidentally offend your friend or have her start thinking she has made the wrong decision to get pregnant in the first place? Can you say, "Oh yeah, you've really blown up! I wonder how long it's going to take to get rid of that weight"? Or add an "Oh you'll be fine. All my friends dropped the baby weight the week after giving birth"? The answer is that unless you're really close, just don't. You want to avoid playing the "expert" here because that can really get on someone's nerves. Remember that you're not the only one with friends who have had children, and you're also not the one who is pregnant now.

Listen or Avoid the Subject

It can be difficult at times, but lending an understanding ear without giving an opinion can often be more than enough. Keep in mind that during pregnancy, a woman's hormones are all over the place. Sometimes she just needs to rant to any poor bugger who will listen. She doesn't really want to hear opinions that will challenge her own when it comes to the baby from someone who hasn't been through it before, as sagely as you might imagine yourself to be from all the friends you have who are mothers, or from all the internet sites you've read. Just chill. Listen if you can bear it or try to avoid the subject altogether.

Don't Compare Your Experiences with Those You Don't Understand

Don't be the friend that compares morning sickness with that time you got really drunk, so you "totally know the feeling." Also, don't try to empathize with situations that are not yours unless the person in your story coped worse. Trust me, no one suffering morning sickness wants to hear "oh but you've got it easy; my friend had morning sickness much worse than you." No, no, no. It doesn't work like that. It's not easy. Don't invalidate the pregnant woman's struggles by saying that others have had it much worse but coped better. They're not going to think, *Oh, you know what, you're right! I should thank my lucky stars that I feel like shit only 23.5 hours out of the day instead of 24. I really am just being a whiner.* Nope. They're going to be thinking, *Fuck you. YOU try this.*

Well, What Can You Talk about Then?

The best thing you can do is chat about other things because it's likely your pregnant friend is tired of always talking about pregnancy and babies. Or if she is inclined to that conversation topic, there is no harm in asking questions without giving opinions unless requested. It's the simple phrases that could make all the difference. For example, "I can't imagine you having a natural birth! With your pain threshold you would die!" If you really felt that way, perhaps you could say something more like, "I couldn't imagine having a natural birth! I don't think *I* would be able to handle the pain." See? Just a little sensitivity can go a long way!

Also, a pregnant friend closer to the finish line is unlikely to want to get dolled up and go out very often—mainly because of the sheer discomfort of shifting so much extra weight, bloatedness, and possibly a squeezed bladder resulting in needing to pee every two minutes. But it doesn't mean that she isn't up for a casual get-together to chat, eat, watch TV—basically do everything, just not out. Proposing popping over with snacks to rant about all the absurd advice she's been given so far can sound like music to a heavily pregnant woman's ears!

Don't Give Bad Advice

It's really difficult to appreciate, but unless you have had to be the primary caregiver for a newborn for a month straight, you don't really understand what it means to be a parent of a newborn. Don't be the friend who gives really bad advice on how to prepare for the baby's arrival. Let's examine some examples of bad advice:

"I don't know why you're stressing so much. You can just wing it when the baby arrives."

There are some things that are better not "winging," like preparing necessities for the baby because *after* the baby arrives, the time a mother has to do the shopping, cooking, organizing, or what not is going to be severely limited.

"I wouldn't worry about getting a breast pump. Nowadays you can just breastfeed anywhere anyway."

This is not the *only* reason women may require a breast pump. There are a myriad of other reasons (e.g., a baby that won't latch, inverted nipples, to encourage the production of more breast milk, or to have a reserve of milk to freeze should the mother return to work . . . just to name a few). If a girl wants to get hold of a pump beforehand, she should—even as a backup because doing research on one after the baby is born is time-consuming and can be stressful.

"No, you won't need to get a Diaper Genie. You can just put your trash out on the balcony and throw nappies out there."

It doesn't matter if the outdoors is just one meter away from the nursery, a Diaper Genie (or other contraption that contains odors) right next to the diaper changer is a game changer. You think the mother or father is going to have time to run outside to throw away that dirty diaper every time they change a nappy? They're not. When the baby does an explosive poo in the middle of the night? No.

"You don't need a bottle sterilizer; you can just boil the bottles" or "You don't really need to sterilize baby bottles!"

It's true you don't need a bottle sterilizer; you can boil bottles. You also don't need a car; you could ride a horse to work. But the time it can save is important to a family with a newborn, and unlike boiling, the situation is one where you can set and forget it. With newborns, it is highly advised that bottles are sterilized. The advice of "you don't need to sterilize bottles" is often with regards to babies older than twelve months. During the first few months of a baby's life, sterilizing is important to avoid the baby being infected with bacteria that could cause diarrhea or vomiting.

"You don't need to get baby bottles because you'll be breastfeeding, right?"

Try not to make the assumption that the expectant mom will be breastfeeding. It's strongly advocated in many countries but in the end, not every mother will choose to breastfeed. On top of that there are many circumstances that may prevent the mother from breastfeeding. Finally, bottles are actually required, even if breastfeeding, in case the mother pumps and stores milk for feeds by somebody else—be it at daycare or while she is getting some sleep of her own. If an expectant mom wants to be prepared for every situation, just let her be. Again, her time to do these things after the baby's arrival is going to be limited.

QUICK QUIZ

Your friend and her husband are discussing how to prepare for the baby. She wants to buy the whole shebang of baby goods. He doesn't think everything is necessary and is trying to convince her to remove items out of the online shopping cart. You happen to be stuck in the middle of this discord. What do you do?

A. Agree with the husband and say, "Don't worry about it; you won't need the Diaper Genie. If you're worried about the smell of diapers, you can put the bin right outside the back door."
B. Agree with the wife and say, "Yes, you should get the Diaper Genie. I've heard it's an absolute lifesaver. You can't do without one!"
C. Butt out and don't say anything. Pop over with a Diaper Genie as a gift the following day.
D. Butt out, stay out. It's none of your business. *Awkward!*

The politically correct answer would be (D). The baby is after all your friend's *and* her husband's and they should be able to make all decisions together without a third party interfering to side with one or the other. There would be nothing wrong with you going with this option. No one would have anything bad to say about you for taking this course of action. However, if you're a great friend, option (C) would be the way to go. You can show your solidarity with your friend through action, provided that it's for relatively small things and not big-ticket items. Oops, you bought it before ever being witness to their little tiff.

Just be prepared for the other half of the couple (in this case, the husband) to never really like or see the point in your gift. *Extravagant, you are!*

PART TWO

THE FIRST WEEKS AFTER THE BABY IS BORN

VISITING IN HOSPITAL

There are generally two camps for visiting the mother in the hospital after the baby is born. First are those who understand how tired a woman is after giving birth and how much she would just cherish this time to recuperate and bond with her baby. Then there are those who feel like they should at least socially make that trip over, if not out of politeness, so as not to disturb the mother when she is sent home with the baby.

Both ways of thinking are totally valid. Keep in mind that hospital policies regarding newborns vary a lot. There are maternity wards that will keep babies in the nursery and allow visitors to see the newborn through the glass window during visiting hours to lower the risk of any visitors passing on germs or diseases. But nowadays to decrease the risk of contamination *within* the nursery there are maternity wards that will ask mothers to keep the baby in their room the entire time, including during visiting hours. Then there are maternity wards that limit the amount of visitors to your room, and those that don't during visiting hours. Just check before you go to understand the situation.

SOME THINGS TO AVOID

Don't Go to Visit If You Are Sick

Even if you just have the sniffles or a sore throat that no one else can detect, just wait until you are well. It's not worth the risk of infecting the mother or the newborn (especially if the baby is kept in the mother's room). The common cold is transmitted by a virus that is spread by little droplets in the air. When these droplets come in contact with the eyes, nose, or mouth of someone else, they can easily become infected.

The virus can spread even when an infected person sneezes, covering their mouth with their hand and then touches things like a phone, a door handle, a *baby* afterwards because the virus can live on these objects for hours after. When a person with a cold looks down on the little baby in their arms and talks to him, these little droplets are also making their way to the baby's eyes, nose, and mouth, so it's better to be prudent and take preventative action by staying away if you're infected. There will be plenty of occasions for you to see the baby after you are well again.

Don't Visit If Your Own Vaccinations Are Not up to Date

Even if you don't show any symptoms of these diseases for which your vaccinations are not up-to-date.

Don't Wake the Baby Under Any Circumstances

This one is quite self-explanatory yet surprisingly it does need to be mentioned. You may have come over from out of town to see this baby, but he's sleeping during your visit to the hospital. Babies need to sleep, so don't wake them up! Even if it's daytime. They generally sleep throughout the entire day.

Don't Insist on Holding the Baby Unless the Mother Hands Him Over or Asks You to Pick Him Up

Remember the innate protectiveness that a woman starts exhibiting during pregnancy? It usually intensifies after the baby is born. This means being hypervigilant regarding germs (no flowers in the room, thanks!) and about the baby feeling any discomfort or fear. Many women experience a real need to physically bond with their baby and skin-to-skin contact has been proven to comfort both mother and child. During the first few days after the baby is born, don't pick up the baby unless the mother hands him over to you or asks you to. The last thing you want is for the baby to be wailing in your arms. That would distress you, the baby, *and* the mother.

SOME THINGS THAT WOULD BE APPRECIATED

Bring Good Food

Good food is always appreciated after giving birth. If there are things that the new mother couldn't eat while pregnant (e.g., cured meat), bring her some of that if you know it's something she likes. Hospital food is often not the best, so something brought from outside would be nice!

Bring Something for the New Mother

New parents often receive a lot of gifts for the newborn, which is practical and nice. Many times the mother who has just been through this whole process of pregnancy and childbirth is then "forgotten" about as people gush over the baby. It's usually only other mothers who remember the feeling of being pushed aside now that the "hard part" is over, while all the focus is now on the baby.

Something nice for the new mother can be as simple and practical as a thermos to keep her coffee hot, make-up, or a bathrobe. It's something for "Mom" to mark the occasion but still reminds her that first and foremost she is also a human woman. As giving and as motherly as we may become, it's always important to feel like a person with needs, desires, and a life or identity outside of that. To be reminded of that is truly lovely.

Keep the Visit Short

When you visit someone who has just given birth, they're often not at their very best. They are more or less recovering from a surgery, whether they had a C-section or not. Everything is a bit uncomfortable. They're having what's like the heaviest period of their life. It hurts to pee if they've given birth naturally. It hurts to cough or laugh if they've had a C-section. Yes, it's a wonderful time but it's also not a glamorous moment, so keep your visit short and sweet unless you're very close or the new mother needs your moral support, in which case she would ask for it.

AT HOME WITH THE BABY

First and foremost, during the first few weeks of life, a healthy newborn does not need anyone else but his or her mom and possibly dad. Period. So when you decide to pop over to the new mother's home, keep in mind that you're there *to help the mother* who is likely to be someone you care about, or are friends with. If you were never friends or were not on good terms to begin with, don't call over to "see the baby." Sadly but truly, the baby doesn't want to see you!

MOST NEW MOTHERS WANT SPACE

Many friends and relatives think that after the mother gives birth, she's going to want or need all the help she can get. So they "pop over" to see what's up. They keep insisting on visiting because they're worried the mother is going to fall into postnatal depression or something. Usually this is all with good intention, but oddly enough during those first few weeks of bringing the baby home, most mothers want to just be left alone with the baby. They want that time to bond and they're in super-protective mode, so the last thing they want is extra germs entering the house getting near their precious baby. Not to mention their hormones start to shift in this super-protective mode and they can get very anxious during this time as they themselves are also entering unfamiliar territory.

SHOULD YOU GET INVOLVED, SEEING AS YOU HAVE MORE EXPERIENCE IN OR AROUND MOTHERHOOD?

Motherhood is a very personal experience that every mother should be able to enter into in whichever way they wish, without judgment or commands from others. Even the coldest person becomes naturally "motherly" after they have given birth to a child because it's nature. So naturally, every mother is also quite innately sure that they will be able to take care of this baby even though it may take a few weeks for them to get the hang of the new responsibility.

During this period, it's doubtful that having an "experienced" mother to look on and give advice at every turn is going to be calming or helpful. Indeed, some women do have this type of relationship with their own mothers, so being hand held every step of the way might be somewhat natural to the dynamic between them. Normally people only take advice from sources they find reliable. If they believe that they themselves turned out well, they may listen to their parent's advice. If they feel there was something lacking in their childhood, they won't. And if you're a mother-in-law don't automatically assume that just because they chose to have a child your son, they think he's perfect or that he was raised perfectly.

Imagine you're about to try cooking a Gordon Ramsay recipe [side note: they always turn out well if you follow the instructions]. You're gathering the ingredients, all the while with your mother-in-law peering over your back. You go to pick up the paprika. "You know it tastes better with dried chili flakes" comes the voice from behind you. You throw the onions in the pan. "You should have chopped those more finely." "What are you doing with those canned tomatoes? They're the wrong brand anyway," "that's far too little salt," "where's the pasta?"

Sounds annoying, doesn't it? Cooking becomes a stressful event under such circumstances. Anyone would feel tense and uncomfortable. It's definitely not an environment conducive to gaining confidence in the kitchen.

Imagine if this continued with a hundred other micromanaging comments before she realized that you were making something completely different and not her traditional Spaghetti Al Ragù. *That* is what unsolicited parenting advice is like.

The same goes even more for friends without kids who pop over to talk about all things baby. Would you want cooking advice from someone who claims to have cooking skills simply because they eat? Probably not.

The first few weeks after giving birth and bringing the baby home can be a bit chaotic. The new mother may just be finding her feet. Not only is this period physically tiring but it can be a period of mental adjustment too. The new mother may be living in a sleep-deprived haze as the baby wakes, cries, wants to be fed, and generally is being a baby. You don't want to add to this chaos by emotionally tiring out the mother. She already realizes that she has little time to herself and needs to begin to understand her life with a newborn. Unsolicited advice disguised as comments or little anecdotes about "what I did was…" or "my friend did…" is not going to help. That word "unsolicited" means a lot there. If it's not asked for, don't give it.

Sometimes you may think that you're just sharing information or 'being there' for the new mom. You're probably genuinely concerned, after all, the woman who was once well put together and bubbly is now wearing maternity tights post maternity all day and is in desperate need of a brush run through her hair. But here is something to think about. When a new mom, clearly in need of some form of assistance declines your offers for help with "don't worry, I've got this", chances are that she is trying to place a boundary back between you that she feels you have overstepped, be it with unsolicited advice, opinions or actions. The same assistance offered from somebody else may be taken with great appreciation.

WHAT NO NEW MOTHER WANTS TO HEAR

There are things no new mother wants to hear. She may not tell you so directly (though don't be surprised to find her distancing herself from you), but these are small things that can be hurtful, if not just plain annoying.

Your Opinion on Whether or Not She Should Be Breastfeeding

In 2020, while I'm writing this, breastfeeding is heavily advocated by many health organizations. However, this does not mean that mothers not breastfeeding for whatever reason should be shamed. Conversely, a mother who wants to breastfeed should not be forced to bottle feed or feed her baby formula because her breastfeeding doesn't fit in with your "schedule" or your belief of what breastfeeding should entail. The decision on breastfeeding lies with the mother and it needs to be respected.

"You can't breastfeed because you have poor eyesight."

Okay, so I wasn't going to add this one here because it's so outrageously stupid, but believe it or not some people actually believe this and pass this information on to new mothers. So I'm putting it out there. This is absolute BS and based on zero science.

"Are you sure you have enough breast milk? The baby is feeding too often!"

This is really none of your business unless you are the baby's mother or doctor. A baby is born and then loses some of his birth weight in the following days. It can take up to two weeks for them to regain up to their birth weight and that is normal. That being said, make sure not to judge a mother for formula feeding either, especially in the beginning. If her milk hasn't "come in" or if her baby has been kept in intensive care for a few days after birth, it is possible that the baby would be formula fed in the first days or weeks. Even if the mother decides afterward to formula feed, that is her choice and she shouldn't be judged for it, as there could be a whole host of reasons as to why.

"Don't worry, the baby won't get sick because you're breastfeeding, and breast milk is loaded with antibodies."

Science has shown that breastfed babies are less likely to get sick. Antibodies in the mother's body are normally passed to the baby to some extent through breast milk. The antibodies in the mother's body are made when she comes into contact with a disease-causing agent. So if she has never come in contact, she may not have those antibodies, and her baby can still become sick if he or she does come into contact with these pathogens. Therefore it is wholly possible that a baby can get sick even if he is being breastfed, and as a newborn it could be very serious.

"The baby needs a routine."

In the first few months after a baby is born, there is no such thing as a routine. Nonetheless, there are those mothers who look back fondly to twenty years ago when they had their babies and remember that for sure their babies had a routine. The incredible thing about the human brain and memory is that it's not all that reliable. Chances are that their babies did not have a routine until much, much later. In the first weeks, babies don't need set eating times or sleeping times. They have little if no concept of time altogether. So when they cry it's often because they want to eat or sleep.

"The baby looks underweight/overweight. Are you sure he's eating enough/not eating too much?"

Hearing this can be a huge anxiety trigger for mothers who might have a baby who is, for example underweight. Even more innocuous comments like "he's so little!" can have the wrong impact. Even if you're just making a passing comment, it can cause a mother to feel inadequate as a provider for her baby, so it's best not to go there. In most developed nations, babies are brought in for frequent check-ups at the hospital or pediatrician. So as long as the parents are taking them to those, everything should be under control.

"You need to put the baby on an eating schedule."

Tying into the above, a few weeks in, a baby does not need to be on an "eating schedule." Especially if he or she is being breastfed, it may seem like the baby is always on the boob. This is completely normal during the early weeks because of the way that breastfeeding works. The more the baby is eating, the more milk is produced. Putting the baby on an "eating schedule" with set times will negatively affect the supply of the mother's breast milk. If the baby is mix fed or formula fed, she still does not need to be on an eating schedule. If the baby finishes a bottle completely, she needs to be fed another until she stops. It's the baby that decides when and how much milk she will drink.

"You need to give the baby chamomile tea so that he/she will sleep."

In the first six months of a baby's life outside of the womb, she needs milk. Breast milk or formula—that is all. It is not advised to give any other type of liquid like water or tea because apart from the fact that you don't want the baby to be full from these nutrient poor liquids and then not feed properly, it is dangerous. A life-threatening condition called water intoxication can occur when you give a baby water. Their kidneys are

84

not yet ready for water and will release sodium with the excess water. This dilution of sodium in their bodies can cause seizures, coma, brain damage, or death. So this is very serious. Please don't give this type of advice to a new mom. You might remember giving your baby water, but it was most likely after your child was over six months old.

"You need to give the baby an enema or a glycerin suppository."

This goes hand in hand with diagnosing the baby and not listening to the mother. The truth is that when this advice comes from somebody who hasn't had a baby in recent years, and therefore can no longer remember the realities of the first few weeks with a newborn, it can be dangerous. Often mothers will forget that their babies did not "regularly" poop at such a young age. They apply the standards we have as adults to a baby's digestive activity. However there are huge differences. First, we're talking about a newborn baby with a digestive tract that is not yet fully developed. Second, the baby is only ingesting milk at this stage, no other food or water. If a baby is breastfed it is absolutely normal for him not to have a bowel movement for seven days. You don't need to give the baby extra "water" or visit a pediatrician. And you don't need to give the baby a micro-enema or a glycerin suppository. If this is the advice you are giving a new parent, stop. Please.

"A bit of prune juice will help with the baby's constipation."

I'm just going to go ahead and say again that the baby's bowel movements need not be your concern. A baby under six months is not going to need anything other than breast milk or formula. If the baby is only a few weeks old, it is generally advised that they are not fed anything other than breast milk or formula because their digestive systems are not yet developed enough.

If they are constipated, your advice should be for the parents to take the baby to a pediatrician. If the pediatrician advises that the parents give the baby prune juice or pear juice, then they will be able to also give advice on how much and how often to do so and how to monitor the effects.

"A bit of lemon and sugar or vinegar will help get rid of the hiccups."

Again, you may remember giving your child lemon and sugar for hiccups, or you may remember a friend doing so. However, it's most likely when the child was older than six months and his kidneys were more developed. Doing so earlier may cause the baby digestive problems.

Hiccups are completely natural and harmless. If they're continuous and frequent enough to cause concern to you (and you're not with the baby as frequently as the parents), chances are that the parents would have already spoken to a doctor about the matter. Don't try to scare the baby or to pull his arms, legs, or tongue to stop the hiccups. Don't advise the baby's parents to do so either.

"You're spoiling the baby by picking him up each time he cries."

In the first few weeks after the baby is born, it is completely unappreciated by mothers when people say things like "Don't pick the baby up when she cries or she will be spoilt with too much affection." First of all, it's factually incorrect—babies at this stage cannot be "spoilt" by affection. Secondly, it's as much for the mother as it is for the child. Many mothers very naturally feel the instinctive need to comfort their crying baby. Did you know that mothers can distinguish *their* baby's crying from other babies? That's how instinctive this reaction is.

As for spoiling, this implies that the baby is manipulative and is crying to manipulate you. They're far too young to understand how to do that at this stage. They're crying because their needs have not been met. Those needs could be physical or emotional. They might be hungry or too hot, lonely or scared just to mention a few possibilities. A parent responding to crying is just trying to meet these needs. And in doing so, they are offering their baby a sense of safety and security. This is very important for babies to develop into independent, confident explorers as children.

"The baby needs to sleep anywhere and get used to sleeping with noise or you can forget about ever having a life again."

This is a myth that creates a lot of confusion for parents of newborns. Many parents are exasperated saying that their babies don't ever want to sleep, yet they take advice like this and expect that their babies will magically fall asleep with the TV on or guests over or out at dinner. When babies sleep in this type of environment with noise and lights, it's often because they're exhausted. Getting them to sleep when they start to show signs of tiredness is a game changer.

When babies sleep more during the day, they sleep more during the night. They're not over-stimulated while they're awake and so they just fall asleep easier. Just about every baby sleep book written after the 1980s will tell you that. You don't need to "tire them out" during the day. Even though this theory might seem logical to you as an adult, it just doesn't work with babies. Babies need to be settled in a quiet, dark room to sleep for their naps, and then they will sleep better through the night too.

"You don't need to change your life for the baby."

Telling a new mother this is ignorant. And if you too are a mother, then probably also arrogant. Of course having a baby is going to change a woman's life— especially if she's breastfeeding. Her life has changed. If what you mean is that there are some things you don't think she should sacrifice, such as going out to an occasional dinner or something, then try to work out a solution with her on how she can do this with a newborn to take care of. Acknowledge the fact that she has had a baby and now has this new role to carry out. Telling her that she doesn't need to change her life doesn't help.

"I want to babysit the baby for a day."

The first few weeks of the baby's life—even the first few months—is a period of time where a baby needs only his/her mother. During this time, often the mother also has a bit of separation anxiety. After all, the baby was inside her body for the past nine months! If you've been excitedly anticipating the birth of this child, be it your grandchild, niece, or nephew, it may be hard to resist, but don't insist on taking the baby away from the mother until the mother is ready to let you. Hinting by showing photos of your friends' babies out with their aunts or grandparents on a day without the parents is only going to make the new mother feel uneasy. Remember that the baby is not yours and imposing a time when you want to take him away from his mother to "spend a day together" is overstepping the boundaries. Just chill and wait until both the mother and baby are ready.

Calling the Baby *"My Baby"*

If it's not your baby, please don't call him that. It may be a term of endearment that you use to convey your love for the child, but it can be frustrating for mothers who went through the whole actual pregnancy and labor process to have the baby. Think of other ways you can convey this adoration.

Diagnosing the Baby with an Illness

One of the most frustrating things that you could do to a new mother is pick up the baby and begin to examine him/her and then diagnose the baby with an illness. Or even colic. Or tummy pains. Or growing pains. Or autism. Or strabismus. Or anything—unless you yourself are a licensed and practicing pediatrician.

K ATIE RECALLS, "When I brought my daughter home, she would cry whenever I let somebody else hold her. Her grandmother didn't want to believe that perhaps the baby just wanted to be in my arms and so instead of giving her back to me continued to try different positions to hold the baby, repeating out loud that it was colic, despite me explaining that it was unfamiliarity. I almost had to wrestle the baby back in my arms. That was definitely frustrating and insensitive. A baby's mother just somehow knows when something is not right and can usually pinpoint it better than anybody else. We don't need you to come and give your theories on what is wrong with our children, especially when they're not asked for."

If you do see something of concern, instead of diagnosing you could suggest that the parents take the baby to their chosen pediatrician.

Giving Advice on How to Deal with a Baby's Condition After Diagnosis

Once again, unless you're a pediatrician or have had a baby recently (aka this generation), then refrain from giving advice on how to deal with a baby's condition after diagnosis—especially if a treatment has been prescribed by the baby's pediatrician. Sometimes the treatment is just to wait. Sometimes it may involve pharmaceuticals. It's the parents' decision whether or not to give their baby medicine, but it can be downright negligent of the parents not to follow the pediatrician's prescribed treatment without discussing with him why so and whether there are other alternatives. So don't encourage that either. For example, if you personally hate taking pharmaceuticals and usually go the naturopath or herbal remedy route, don't encourage the mother to give the baby a naturopathic remedy for a condition for which the pediatrician has prescribed a pharmaceutical.

A NOTE ON "NATUROPATHIC REMEDIES"

Just because it's "natural" doesn't mean that herbal medicine can't be harmful. The herbal products industry is less regulated than the pharmaceutical industry, and considering that there are no standards and no legal body to control the contents, safety, or efficacy of herbal products, they're not necessarily better. Herbal remedies are also often slow in their efficacy if they work at all. For example, if a child has oral thrush, he could be on an herbal treatment for weeks or it could be cleared up in a day with an antifungal medication.

Giving Your Opinion on Whether the Baby Is Wearing Too Much, or Too Little

Unless the issue has been clearly overlooked, there is no need to give your opinion on how the baby is dressed. If you've been outdoors walking on a winter's day, and find a baby bundled up please don't begin to tell the parents that the baby is wearing too much because *you* feel hot. Babies' bodies are different from adults. Because they have a much higher surface area to volume ratio, they lose heat up to four times faster and are not so easily able to regulate their own body temperature.

Another annoyingly incorrect concept is "If the baby is dressed like this already in autumn, what will she wear in winter?" Cold weather is cold weather. It doesn't matter which "season" it is labeled. If the baby needs mittens on a 9-degree Celsius autumn's day, then she needs mittens. If 9 degrees is normally the temperature in winter, then yes, she will be bundled up in "winter" gear in autumn. It's not about "fashion" with babies; it's about health and logic. If winter temperatures drop down to 0 degrees then she will need to be bundled up even more.

Stress and the New Mom

There are many easily avoidable things that can cause a new mother to feel uncomfortable. Apart from unsolicited advice and opinions regarding the baby or the mother's health, there are a few other factors that should also be taken into consideration.

Smoking

Smoking around the baby, or smoking and then holding and kissing the baby, touching cigarettes and then picking up the baby is just inconsiderate. Don't do it.

Make-up

If you wear a lot of make-up, don't snuggle with the baby or kiss the baby with your lipstick, even if the mother does it. Even if your make-up is "chemical free" or "organic," it's better to err on the safe side. If you really must kiss the baby, then test the waters first and say something like "I really would like to give the baby a kiss but I'm wearing lipstick, so I don't want to leave a big red mark!" to which the mother may say "Yeah, next time." Or she may say, "Don't worry about it." Whatever her response, don't push it. For example, if she says, "Yeah, next time," don't add "Oh wait! But you do it all the time." Because it's *her* baby.

Plastic, Aluminum Foil & Choking Hazards

Babies go through a stage of putting everything in their mouths. And many also happen to be able to spot the tiniest pieces of rubbish (think those plastic fasteners that attach tags to clothing and toys to packaging, dead insects, small rocks, pieces of aluminium, staples etc.) within their reach. By the time they're dextrous enough, these bits will be going in their mouths for a taste test and some become choking hazards while others, though may go down, are not good for our bodies. So when you know there's a baby around, try to make sure you're not doing something that might involve these pieces flying everywhere such as excitedly helping the mother to de-tag all the babies clothing by pulling on one side, and causing that little, usually transparent, asshole of a piece of plastic fastener on the back to then go missing. If you don't find it together, it's more than likely new-mom will be worried about it. And the point is to help her stress less, not more.

THE EFFECTS OF STRESS

Stress Negatively Affects Breast Milk Supply

In the first few weeks, it's very important to not unknowingly cause the new mom stress. A huge reason for this, especially for women who are breastfeeding, is that stress leads to the release of cortisol, adrenaline, and norepinephrine in the body. Increased levels of cortisol in the body is known to decrease the supply of breast milk and that is some serious shit for a new mother who is trying to exclusively breastfeed. In this day and age, mothers are heavily encouraged to breastfeed where possible, so there are definitely the feelings of guilt and inadequacy to provide when she doesn't have enough milk. This creates a vicious cycle of stress and low milk supply. You definitely don't want to add to the stress part of that.

Stress Affects the Quality of Breast Milk

Apart from just being bad for the mother emotionally and physically, increased levels of cortisol has been linked to increased cortisol in her breast milk. This makes its way to the baby and is called secondhand cortisol. Research has shown that babies with higher levels of cortisol in their systems cry more easily and are more agitated in unfamiliar situations.[5] Which once again, adds to that vicious cycle of additional stress to the mother, and lower milk supply.

Stress Affects the Baby

Another important reason to not add stress to the newborn's mother is that research has shown that infants not only are able to sense their mother's stress, evidenced by physiological changes such as increased heart rates to mirror that of their mother's, but it also shows that there are measurable behavioral responses to this increase in stress. In this research, infants with

---

[5] Glynn, Laura & Davis, Elysia & Schetter, Christine & Chicz-Demet, Aleksandra & Hobel, Calvin & Sandman, Curt. (2007). Postnatal maternal cortisol levels predict temperament in healthy breastfed infants. *Early human development. 83.* 675-81. 10.1016/j.earlhumdev.2007.01.003.

stressed mothers became more reluctant to interact with strangers.[6]

So, stressing out the new mom is not good for her or the baby. This is why it's so important for family and loved ones to actively work hard not to overstep any boundaries—be it imposing on the new mom's time, on her method of taking care of the baby, on her decisions regarding how she will feed the baby, when the baby should be sleeping, or any of the things that don't actively concern you. As much as you may feel you are helping with your suggestions, try to keep them to yourself unless the new mother has actively sought your advice.

BONDING

After bringing home the baby from the hospital, the first few weeks are for the parents to bond with the child, especially the mother. These days it's general practice that the child will be placed skin-to-skin on the mother's chest immediately after birth because this bonding experience is so important for the baby and

---

[6] Waters, S. F., West, T. V., & Mendes, W. B. (2014). Stress contagion: physiological covariation between mothers and infants. *Psychological science*, *25*(4), 934–942.

also for the mother. It's so primal and part of the magic of having a child. Among other benefits, skin-to-skin releases hormones in the mother's body that help breastfeeding and mothering. It also helps regulate the baby's heartbeat and temperature. So in the first few weeks it's important to allow the mother to continue this bonding experience with her child, and for the father also, who up to this point may feel a little left out in the whole bonding experience.

Now is absolutely not the time to insist that the mother start leaving the baby with the grandparents, childcare, or whoever for the baby to "get used to" being with other people. Nobody needs to be worried that the baby is being too attached to the mother at this stage. At this point in life of course she's going to be attached to the person with whom she is most familiar and who feeds her. That's survival instincts, a part of human nature. A small baby needs that sense of security.

BREASTFEEDING

Breastfeeding is a time when a mother can bond with her baby. Lately due to the benefits of breastfeeding it is heavily advised that almost all mothers try to breastfeed their babies until they reach at least twelve months old. The World Health Organization (WHO) even advises through two years old and up.

A mother's milk may not come in or be sufficient in the first couple of days after giving birth and the baby may have to take formula milk. However, this doesn't mean that she will never have enough milk to feed her baby. The way that breastfeeding works is that the more the baby suckles at the breast, the more the message will be sent through hormones for the mother's body to create more milk. It's just another one of life's little miracles. So the more the baby feeds, the more milk will be produced to satisfy that demand.

If the mother still wishes to breastfeed, even if you see that it is difficult for her to continue doing so (e.g., feeding throughout the day, cracked nipples, she's tired), let her keep trying by continuing to attach the baby before the baby takes a bottle. If she prefers to feed her baby formula instead, there is absolutely no shame in that either. Fed, whether breastfed or formula fed, is best. This is however a section for navigating a woman who is breastfeeding, so here are some tips.

A SHORT LIST OF DON'TS WHEN IT COMES TO A MOTHER HAVING BREASTFEEDING DIFFICULTIES:

- Don't discourage her and tell her that she doesn't have enough milk.
- Don't tell her to just use a breast pump while you feed the baby formula. The stimulation of breast pumps does not mimic the results from her actual baby feeding on the breast when it comes to milk production, as much as the breast pump marketers try to have you believe. It's just not true. A baby can feed at a much faster rate than a pump can express.
- Don't tell her to switch to formula because "some women just don't produce milk." If she wants to make that decision she will make it. Try to help her by alleviating the things that may be causing her stress: others bringing breastfeeding up as a conversation topic, allowing others to impose "you should" on her, not engaging in any stressful activities or

conversations. This could be all the help she needs.

- Don't sit there and watch her try to breastfeed. More than likely, this is not at all as supportive as you think it is. It's more stressful for the mother if anything.

Finally, just because she's feeding the baby for what seems like "all the time," doesn't mean there isn't enough milk being produced and that she should be encouraged to start formula feeding. Newborns feed at irregular times, and when they are hungry they will cry until fed. If the mother doesn't have enough milk, then the baby will most likely unlatch and start crying. Otherwise, sometimes babies do cluster feed (feed every twenty minutes or so) and this is normal.

Furthermore, it needs to be understood that a breastfed baby cannot be "overfed." In fact, neither can a formula fed baby. Babies self-regulate; they stop when they are full. So if a baby is on the breast for what seems like forever, it's normal. Please don't tell a mother of a newborn that she is overfeeding her baby. And if the baby is feeding at the middle of the night, this is also completely normal. You can't "schedule" a baby's feeding times at this age. This is just the nature of breastfeeding. It's a full-time job in itself during the first few months of a baby's life.

It cannot be stressed enough that stress is a huge factor when it comes to a mother's milk supply, so try to be supportive by informing yourself with the latest information from trusted, accredited sources, not obscure websites or retired pediatricians who no longer practice.

HOW CAN YOU BE HELPFUL TO SOMEONE WHO IS BREASTFEEDING?

- Offer privacy. Sitting there and staring at her breasts, even if you're sympathizing over her cracked nipples, is a no unless you're a lactation specialist or someone with whom the mother is seeking counsel on how to breastfeed.
- Bring her some water to drink because breastfeeding leaves you thirsty. Water, not wine or beer!

TIPS FOR HUSBANDS

BONDING WITH YOUR BABY

When a baby is born, the father in the delivery room holds the baby for the first time and falls in love immediately when this tiny creature wraps its hand tightly around his finger. Tears of joy flow and immediately this baby is the most beautiful thing that the father has ever seen. This is the scene we're meant to believe carries out every time, for every father with half a beating heart. I'm calling BS on that. Not on that particular scenario, which would be wonderful, but on the fact that we're meant to believe that is *the one and only* scenario that is supposed to play out. That fathers are supposed to naturally feel this immediate bond with their offspring. No. There is such a high expectation for a father to feel this way, that even the baby's mother may feel hurt if he doesn't have this type of instant reaction to the birth of their baby. So I'm not saying fake it, but if this isn't your first reaction, maybe fake it a little?

The reality is that many new fathers don't feel this connection or bond with the infant immediately. If the mother is breastfeeding, the first few weeks may see the baby on the boob feeding a great deal of the time that he is awake. For the father, it may feel like there is no time to "bond" with your child!

If the baby isn't breastfeeding, the bond between a father and his child may still take time. That is totally normal. As the husband, try to help out and involve yourself in taking care of the baby as much as you can. Not only will this be super helpful for your wife, but also it's during these moments that the bond between you and your child is built.

Just a note that if you think having a baby is not going to require you to change your life in some ways, then you're in for a rude awakening. Prepare yourself for nights in, longer preparation times before heading out the door, and kid-friendly restaurants and holidays. These all come part in parcel with having children.

HELPING YOUR WIFE

As we've covered, the first few weeks after a baby is born, your wife is in a very protective mode, and for good reason. The baby's immune system is not yet developed enough to handle germs. This means that she probably doesn't want a lot of people to be touching the baby. Definitely nobody needs to be touching the baby's face or hands at this stage. You need to help your wife out here. Many visitors won't think twice about these things. In some cultures people may pick even up, kiss, or stroke the baby's face without asking.

A lot of mothers feel paranoid about seeming pedantic about this, though inside their blood is boiling. Sadly, there are many cases of newborns who are infected with diseases in "first world" countries, with some dying because of negligent people kissing babies or not washing their hands before handling them.[7] In the wake of COVID-19, this should now be obvious to everyone yet it cannot be said enough. Even in the best of times, it's distressing to every new mother. So step in here and tell your visitors, especially if they're your side of the family or friends, to wait until the baby is just a bit bigger, or at least ask them to wash their hands first.

---

[7] Truong, K. Refinery29, *Why This Mom Is Warning Parents Not to Let People Touch Their Babies* [online], Vice Media Group, Published July 19, 2017, accessed March 30, 2020
https://www.refinery29.com/en-us/2017/07/163983/mom-warns-touching-babies

WHAT ARE SOME WAYS YOU CAN HELP?

In many cultures, after a healthy baby is born, apart from the 2–5 days the mother spends in hospital afterward, everything is about the baby. Hardly anybody checks in on the mother and realizes that giving birth is exhausting. The delivery, then the changes in hormones, plus the sheer exhaustion from being pregnant and physically carrying so much more weight are all things that make it reasonable for your wife to ask that you help with tasks that don't require a breast with milk in it. At least for the first few weeks.

You may or may not know this but your wife, whether she had a C-section or vaginal delivery, is bleeding heavily for up to four weeks after giving birth. What does that actually mean? It means she probably doesn't feel like going out on long trips, having to take care of a baby and changing a sanitary pad every few hours.

In many Asian cultures, there is a "confinement period" that is generally practiced to this day. This is a time when the new mother rests and stays home or indoors for thirty days post-delivery. She is not to do anything except eat healthily, rest, and recuperate. Staying at home for so long can make anyone suffer a bit of cabin fever and possibly also depression, so lately this rule has been relaxed. New moms can leave the house but they are supposed to recuperate. This has become a billion-dollar industry in Asia with resort-like facilities catering to this clientele. So just keep this in mind. When your wife asks you to pick up dinner, you're winning compared to if she were to ask you to pick up the bill for one of those resorts!

Let's take a look at some helpful pointers for how (without spending the big bucks) you can earn those brownie points and get your wife/partner physically and more so, mentally, back into fighting form to tackle this thing called parenthood together.

Don't Say the Baby Is Ugly

Under no circumstance should you say out loud to anybody, except maybe yourself and your psychologist, that the baby your wife so painstakingly created in her body over the past nine months is ugly. In the first few weeks after birth, that kind of comment won't be funny or appreciated at all. Keep it to yourself. All babies change and sometimes it's not for months until they are cute.

Be Emotionally Supportive During This Period

As a husband and a father, you are now more able to engage in this whole experience of being a parent together with your wife. Oftentimes women begin to place the baby first in every circumstance, at the detriment of her relationship with her husband. The key to remember is that together you and your wife are a team on this adventure of parenthood. Communication and action to show that commitment to each other is paramount. Try to understand why she may be hesitant to be out and about with the baby in the first few weeks. Hopefully reading this book will be able to give you plenty of insight into what she may be going through.

Cook or Prepare the Meals

If you can't cook, then it would be highly appreciated if you somehow got everyone fed decently. With the convenience of "ready to eat" meals at supermarkets, food delivery services, and restaurants that offer take-out, it's really not a big ask that you somehow get everyone who is not a baby fed the first few weeks after the newborn is brought home.

Don't Expect to Go Out to Dinner or Social Events in the First Few Weeks Unless Your Wife Is Up for It

If you have a fussy baby, dinners at restaurants or social events can turn out to be more stressful than enjoyable. Play it by ear because some babies are super chill while others can be a bit more of a handful. The idea is very sweet. Maybe you want to take your wife out for a nice meal to make her feel relaxed, special, and loved. But with a fussy baby you probably won't achieve your objective and at this stage she may not be ready to leave the baby—however briefly—with anyone else. Perhaps a dinner in with her favorite take-out could do the trick instead.

Lower Your Expectations of How Organized Your House Should Be Unless You Can Singlehandedly Keep It Organized

You've got a baby now. That and the sanity of your wife are the priorities.

Learn Your Part Well

This includes how to make a bottle from frozen breast milk or formula, how to sterilize bottles, how to wash and warm bottles. How long are bottles good for? How to assemble each type of bottle. How to use the sterilizer. Which parts are needed for which breast pump? How to change a baby's diaper. How to wash a baby, how to clean the baby's belly button. These are all the things you can help with, especially if your wife is breastfeeding and spending half of her waking life doing so. It's one thing to carry out these tasks when asked and instructed by your wife each time they need to be carried out, but it's a completely different thing to *learn* this as your part. That way she doesn't need to talk you through step by step what is needed while she could be doing something else like trying to put the baby down to sleep after a feed.

Don't be one of the fathers who are self-conscious or embarrassed in public with their baby when it comes to situations like crying, an explosive poo, or a stroller that gets stuck or is difficult to drive. Just do what's required and take it all in stride. Nobody feels 100 percent confident about what they're doing. And if anyone's judging you from afar, who cares. They clearly have nothing better to do with their time and it really speaks volumes more about them than it does about you. Don't take yourself too seriously. As cool, calm, and collected as you may want to look with perhaps a designer stroller with gold-rim wheels and a designer baby bag to boot, everyone knows that's just a façade for the realities of parenthood.

Don't take yourself or being the "perfect dad" too seriously because that attitude can ruin your experiences out and about with your baby. Once you get over this mental hurdle, you will be able to really respond to your child and take care of what is actually important in a situation, such as properly strapping the baby into the car seat instead of caring about the car that is waiting for your parking spot, or cleaning an explosive diaper efficiently instead of pulling faces of disgust just in case anyone who happens to walk past imagines that calmness must indicate that you've gone so feral you're no longer deterred by foul odors. That's in your head. If anyone's sticking around to watch at all, it's more likely in sheer admiration… and perhaps a bit of sympathy.

Post Baby Blues, Postpartum Anxiety, Postpartum Depression and Postpartum Psychosis Vs. You Really Just Being a Shit Partner

Because of hormones adjusting and basically going wild at this stage, the new mother may experience some form of the "baby blues" or anxiety. She may be joyous at one moment and crying the next. She may feel overwhelmed and anxious, not eat properly, and be emotionally fragile. For many mothers this anxiety includes the feeling that they can't trust anyone with the baby, yet knowing that they also can't do everything themselves. They worry about the baby all the time, the baby crying can cause their cortisol to spike; leaving the house with the baby seems stressful. On top of this her own life as she knew it before giving birth has taken a backseat.

It's a lot to process and can cause even the most alpha female to experience the odd feeling of panic or sense of being overwhelmed. But this shouldn't completely take away her ability to function. She is after all finding her feet. The feeling that this baby who was once inside her is now outside, and therefore also out of her control, can cause anxiety. But that's *normal* and usually passes after a couple of weeks.

Please read this entire section really well if you think that it's possible your wife is suffering from postpartum anxiety or symptoms of the baby blues that are lingering for longer than two weeks. Is she actually mentally unstable or are you being a shit husband? Does she have shitty people around her stressing her out? Could you do better? Could the conditions improve to alleviate some of her stress and anxiety? If the answer really is no, then encourage her to see a doctor. Often people with postpartum depression can't recognize it in themselves. The chemicals in their brain have gone all over the place and you need to help them out.

Postpartum depression (PPD) is a serious and potentially dangerous condition that affects some new mothers and should not be taken lightly. If your wife is showing signs of PPD, encourage her to talk to her midwife or OB/GYN immediately to get help and treatment. The signs of postpartum depression, and the more rare and severe condition of postpartum psychosis, as listed by the Mayo Clinic are[8]:

---

[8]MAYO CLINIC, *Postpartum Depression* [online] , Published by Mayo Foundation for Medical Education and Research, 2020, Accessed 29 March, 2020. [https://www.mayoclinic.org/diseases-conditions/postpartum-depression/symptoms-causes/syc-20376617]

SIGNS OF POSTPARTUM DEPRESSION

- Depressed mood or severe mood swings
- Excessive crying
- Difficulty bonding with your baby
- Withdrawing from family and friends
- Loss of appetite or eating much more than usual
- Inability to sleep (insomnia) or sleeping too much
- Overwhelming fatigue or loss of energy
- Reduced interest and pleasure in activities you used to enjoy
- Intense irritability and anger
- Fear that you're not a good mother
- Hopelessness
- Feelings of worthlessness, shame, guilt, or inadequacy
- Diminished ability to think clearly, concentrate, or make decisions
- Restlessness
- Severe anxiety and panic attacks
- Thoughts of harming yourself or your baby
- Recurrent thoughts of death or suicide

SIGNS OF POSTPARTUM PSYCHOSIS

- Confusion and disorientation
- Obsessive thoughts about your baby
- Hallucinations and delusions
- Sleep disturbances
- Excessive energy and agitation
- Paranoia
- Attempts to harm yourself or your baby

ADVICE FOR EVERYONE ELSE IN A NEW MOTHER'S ORBIT

NOTES TO MOTHERS OF NEW MOTHERS

Congratulations on becoming a grandmother! If this is your first grandchild, then I'm glad to have gotten to you early. The goal is that you can start the assumption of this new title armed with the refreshed knowledge of the inner-workings of a new mom and therefore be there for her in helpful ways. If you're already a grandmother, you may have encountered situations or be in one where you can't make sense of why your daughter may be behaving the way she is toward you now that she herself is now a mother. Let's try to avoid that from happening again by exploring the potential causes. Here is your cheat sheet. So without further adieu -

New Mothers Can Be Snappy Assholes

The first few weeks after your daughter brings her new baby home, she may ask you to stay with her family to help out. Or she may call you for help or advice. I'm not saying drop your life and run to assist, but it's often greatly appreciated when a woman's mother can be there when she's just had a baby. A big reason for this is that usually she knows what she can expect from her mother. Even if she feels like you could have done a better job, she *knows* to expect what you will say or do. Those small disagreements can be hashed out on the spot instead of held in to fester into a deep resentment (which may be the case with anybody else).

A new mother knows her own mother will forgive her for lashing out at her, for the meltdowns, the sometimes not-so-polite requests for help, or snappiness. This is all part and parcel with the changes in hormones, as well as psychological adjustment to becoming a mother and mostly due to the utter lack of sleep a new mother often suffers. As one new mother explains, "With sufficient sleep, I can do everything. It's this constant sleep deprivation that makes even the simplest tasks difficult."

Remember That You're Not There Just to Spend Time with the Baby

If your daughter lives in a different city and you do go to help out during the first few, sometimes difficult weeks, remember that you are there to help your daughter find her feet during this transition period. You're not there just to "spend time with the baby." Although boundaries should be considered when staying in somebody else's home, remember that you're fully independent too. Don't expect to be treated as a visiting guest to be taken out to see the local sights, then sit back with the baby while your daughter prepares the meals. You need a shift in perspective, which is that your own precious daughter just gave birth and now needs time to bond with her baby and recuperate.

Chances are your daughter has called for your help because she cannot do all the things she used to before the baby arrived. Try to pick up that slack while she spends this important time nursing, bonding, and resting. Small actions like throwing a load of laundry in the wash, doing the grocery shopping, making herbal teas while she is nursing, or even just being there for conversation go highly appreciated. If she needs help with the baby himself, she will ask you. Don't go in guns blazing. Remind yourself that this is *her* opportunity to be a mother.

POST-DELIVERY NOTES FOR SISTERS AND BROTHERS

Be Mindful of Overstepping Boundaries

The first few weeks after the baby is born is the period when the new mother is finding her feet at home. If you're close with your sister, whether you've had children or not, you might want to drop by and visit frequently to see the new baby or to check in on your sister. Just note that during this period of time, the baby's father may also feel like he needs to bond with the baby, and so you being over all the time can make him feel uncomfortable.

Remember that the baby really only needs his mother at this stage. Dropping by as a courtesy visit to see the baby is one thing, but dropping by to try to bond with the baby during this phase can be overstepping your boundaries.

Be There for Your Sister

If your sister asks you to drop by for some moral support while her husband is at work or while he's away or even while he is home, that's a different thing.

Maybe she just wants to relax, chat, rant, and feel like a person rather than a zombie/milk factory. Check in with *her* to make sure that she is okay. Alleviate some of her other pressures if you can to allow her time to bond with her child. At this stage, be there for your sister, not for the baby.

If you have a rocky relationship with your sister and she lives in a different city and will need to host you while you visit, it would probably be best that you don't visit unless you make other arrangements for yourself while you are in town. The last thing you should do is stress out a new mother. If you're there just to see the baby (versus to support your sister), then it may be better to visit a few months after the baby is born. That way your sister has time to get used to life with the new baby, can probably get a bit more sleep, and would likely be less prone to being snappy, provoked, or irritable. This would be beneficial to both of you.

PARENTS-IN-LAW

Don't Get the First Few Weeks Wrong

The relationship between mother-in-law and daughter-in-law is quite often tricky. That's a universal truth and more so in some cultures than others. Navigating the first few weeks after the birth of your new grandchild in a sensitive way is very important because if you get this wrong, it could damage your relationship with the child's mother to the point where she will be able to strongly affect your relationship with her baby in the future.

Try to remember what it was like when you had your first child. Did you want your mother-in-law there all the time? Or was it your mother? Because those are often two very different relationship dynamics. More often than not, new mothers when they want help at all, prefer the guidance of their own parents with whom they grew up. Everything coming from the mother-in-law may seem more judgmental or critical. Just weeks after the baby is born, the mother is going through a hormonal shift so you need to be very aware of her hyper-protective state. Don't mention anything in the way of taking her baby away from her, even just for a few hours because you think she could use the rest. Don't insist even if you entirely mean well. It could come off the wrong way. Remember, she's in super protective, bonding mode. If you want to help, volunteer to do other things.

ROBERTA RECOUNTS, "When I had my son, I had just taken him home from the hospital when my mother-in-law asked me when she could spend a day with him. She proceeded to show me photos of her friend with her one-month-old grandchild out on a 'grandma and me day' together and told me that I had to let her take my baby to show all her friends. I felt like my baby was a 'show and tell' object and at the same time I felt like I was just chopped liver. If she wanted to show her friends her grandchild, it would have made more sense to ask if I could bring the baby by when she had her friends over! He was just born a few days earlier!"

Unfortunately for a Mother-In-Law, Everything Can Be Misconstrued

It can be difficult to see your daughter-in-law struggling during the first few weeks without stepping in and doing something. But again, remember this is a sensitive period. If the baby is crying and the mother is attempting to calm him down, keep in mind that it could be possible that he's not used to your presence or the mother is more stressed by your presence and that is being passed onto the baby. Or it could be just that he's a baby. Don't whisk the baby away in your arms to calm him down. You're unfamiliar to him and chances are it will cause him to become less calm. And don't forget the mother is in hyper-protective and bonding mode. You overtaking in such a way is overstepping boundaries, good intentions or not, and can lead to a lot of resentment from the mother who may feel like you are taking this opportunity of "motherhood" away from her. Or that you're judging her. Or that you are simply stressing her out during what should be a beautiful time in her life.

Stay sensitive to the fact that the mother is the actual mother of the child and not just a by-product that comes along with *your* grandchild because it can *feel* like that for a new mother. If you never got along with your daughter-in-law, then get ready to not be a big part of her child's life—even though it is also your son's child too. It doesn't matter if you think that is wrong. Her baby grew in her body, so it's her prerogative.

If you *do* get along well with your daughter-in-law, then just be very aware of what she's going through at this stage and keep what you say and do in check during these initial weeks. A little comment without the right rapport can unknowingly produce the wrong effect. Even a small comment to your son about what they should or should not be doing needs to be avoided. Let them do them and parent on their own terms. You'll have plenty of time ahead to spoil your grandchild.

BROTHERS AND SISTERS-IN-LAW

Your brother and his wife just had their first child, which makes you an uncle or an aunt! Maybe for the first time too. There are a lot of things brothers and sisters-in-law need to keep in mind, especially if this is their *first* niece or nephew. If you don't have children, then try to be emotionally attuned to what your brother and especially his wife may be feeling about the things you do during this period, so as to not accidentally step beyond the line of being helpful to being annoying.

All Kids Are Different

When a person has a baby, there's a shift in understanding. All babies are different in their own ways and somehow mothers just feel oddly connected with their child. Don't give unsolicited advice on what the mother should do with a colicky baby, or a fussy baby, or a baby that won't feed or poop or sleep unless you've been through the same thing with your own child and you came across a solution that worked for you. Definitely don't insist that a mother do something that you have not already tried yourself with your child.

NINA, A FIRST-TIME MOTHER, had a colicky baby. In the first few days after bringing the baby home, her sister-in-law, who didn't have children, would drop over each day for hours just to "see the baby" and offer her advice. "She told me, 'You need to put the baby on a feeding schedule. I remember that my friend's baby was also crying all the time until she put him on a feeding schedule. Yes. You must look it up.' When I told her that we were going for a routine visit to the pediatrician that afternoon, she still insisted. 'Well then the pediatrician will put her on a schedule and that will fix everything.' I countered with the fact that I was breastfeeding and all doctors and sources say that breastfeeding should be on demand. And she had the gall to say to me, 'No, the doctor will give you a feeding schedule for sure. You'll see.' It was so frustrating. I felt judged, criticized, and belittled all at once."

Clearly, don't be like Nina's sister-in-law. Whether or not she meant to make Nina feel that way, her insistent advice, which came from zero research or firsthand experience, was received in a bad way. She may have *thought* she was being helpful, but when the stakes are *your own* baby, you wouldn't be so keen to try something so against all of the advice humankind as a collective has developed to date.

Respect the Mother as the Baby's Mother

Another point to be aware of is the mother is the baby's mother and she deserves respect when it comes to all things to do with her baby. This means that if you have a question regarding the baby, it should be directed to the baby's mother (aka your sister-in-law) or your brother. And that doesn't mean that it should be directed to your sister-in-law and if you don't get the response you wanted, then turn to your brother.

AGAIN, POOR NINA was feeding her three-week-old baby when her sister-in-law popped over one afternoon. Upon seeing that Nina was feeding the baby formula now, she told her that she needed to give the baby a bottle of water or chamomile tea instead of "all the chemicals" that were in formula milk. "She insisted," says Nina, "and by that time I was already fed up with all of her advice that I didn't even bother backing up my rebuttal with research. I simply said, 'No, I will not be giving her water or tea instead of formula,' to which she just turned her back to me, looked at her brother and said in Italian, 'You know you have to give the baby water, right?' I was livid. She absolutely disregarded my role as the mother, overstepped her boundaries, and insulted me in the process. I had never felt so disrespected in my life! I never talked to her about my child or let her see my child without me after that. Her audacity to overrule what I was saying made me not trust her to follow my instructions if I were ever to leave my child with her."

Make sure you give the mother of the child respect. If you have the baby in your arms and he starts crying while the mother is there, then hand the baby back to the mother. Don't look at your own mother and ask what to do while the baby's actual mother is there. You should be asking her. Furthermore, if the mother of the baby says to stop doing something, don't then look to somebody else to check if what your sister-in-law said is correct and whether you should follow her instruction. You either follow the instructions or give the baby back. It's that simple. If the mother asks for the baby back, do not under *any* circumstances insist that you will stop the baby from crying and refuse to pass the baby back to his mom. I have heard of this happening and just the thought alone would make any mother of a newborn furious. Remember that newborns just want their moms. They may simply be crying because *you're* the one holding them instead of their mother.

Boundaries and Your Changing Relationship with Your Brother

Another note on changing roles relates to your brother now becoming a father. Don't condescend your brother's parenting. Some older siblings always see their brothers as the family dope. If this is you, please keep in mind that the child is his and not yours. He or his wife will be able to determine what parenting style they will adopt. This is not your place to condescend, reprimand, or cast judgment—especially if you don't have children.

Obviously don't be overbearing, particularly in those first few weeks after the baby is born. Even if you have a good relationship with your sister-in-law, it's likely that she will want some alone time with her newborn and her husband. During this time many mothers go through a hormonal shift and become very protective of their baby. They don't want any new germs stemming from people coming to touch, kiss, hold, or even breathe on the baby. Of course the customary short visit is totally fine, but it's best to keep it short. Extend your sincere offer to help whenever needed (if that's the case), and let that be that.

FRIENDS OR RELATIVES WITH CHILDREN

Remember how you were the first few weeks after bringing your firstborn home? It's almost never an easy adjustment and not everyone reacts the same. The experience of a new mother can vary from utter joy and a feeling of fulfillment to anxiety, exhaustion, and possibly depression. Usually it's a mix of these feelings depending on the time or the situation at hand. During those moments of anxiety, if the new mother reaches out with a comment of despair, or an indication that she is not doing so well, your comments and encouragement can make all the difference. Here are some examples of simple reassurance that may seem cliché but are super appreciated by mothers who somehow feel inadequate or overwhelmed:

- "You've got this, mamma!"
- "Hang in there!"
- "You're doing a fantastic job."

These comments bear weight when you yourself are a parent because you've been there; you know what it takes to be a parent. You know and see what they're going through and you think they're doing just fine.

Ladies, when you're at a loss for what to say, it can be difficult to hold back on giving the advice that you heard when you were a new mom—even if you *know* that the advice was downright bogus. You know what I'm talking about! *Sleep when the baby sleeps... Resume your life as normal and just bring the baby out with you; he'll sleep like a baby...* If you can't elaborate on how exactly this worked for you (because it most likely *didn't*, and if it did then probably less than a handful of times), then refrain from giving this type of advice! Think clearly on what really worked for you and offer that or nothing instead.

FRIENDS OR RELATIVES WITHOUT CHILDREN

Friends that pretend to be baby experts because they have other friends with babies are unbearable. You're really not an expert until you have been the main caretaker for a child for over one week straight. No, one week is quite doable. Try one month.

It's a mistake to think that you know because you have "so many friends" who've had children and they did this or that and their children are this or that. If you've ever used social media you know that people only publicize their best moments. You don't know what's actually going on because you don't have a backstage pass to their everyday lives. It goes without saying then, that you shouldn't pass judgment or be critical on material with which you don't have firsthand experience.

If you've taken care of other people's children before, what you may have forgotten is that perhaps they were much older. What's a couple months difference? In "baby time" it may as well be years. For example, in the first few months, babies develop so quickly that a baby at two months is completely different to a baby at four months. Someone who once took care of a five-month-old would have to re-train and reframe their mind for taking care of a two-month-old. It's completely different, and vice versa. That's why giving advice on other people's experiences may *seem* correct—after all their babies were "around this age" too—but could be way off the mark.

That doesn't mean that you can't be there for your friend who has now become a mother. In fact, the company you can offer may be a welcome detachment from *baby this* and *baby that* going on all day in the new mom's world. Without being overly dismissive of the fact that she's just had a baby, you can coo over the baby and still talk about *other* things like she is a well-rounded adult with interests outside of whether her baby is feeding enough and how she might get him to sleep through the night.

PART THREE

THE FIRST YEAR

MOM GUILT

Mom guilt is real and there are so many iterations of it. A mother might feel guilty for not being able to breastfeed her baby, for not having the means to buy the best stroller, for not knowing exactly what the "right" way to raise a baby is, or it may hit simply when the baby cries.

Another less talked about way first-time moms feel guilty is when they don't spend enough "quality" time with their babies. During the first year, a baby develops so much that the changes feel like they're happening every day. A mother usually wants to be there for all the changes, but then they are also there as the primary caregiver (feeding the baby, settling the baby to sleep, cleaning up after the baby), possibly taking care of the household, and probably also working. The amount of time that all these other tasks take is severely under-tallied. The sheer amount of laundry, cleaning, cooking that gets done is almost a full-time job in itself. And that is said without exaggeration. So when a mother has a few minutes with the baby just to "play," she cherishes that. Surprisingly, during that moment of relative "calm," she doesn't need or really want you to come and help take care of the baby because that's *her* time to bond with the child in a different way other than doing the necessities.

If you're the father, don't come and take the baby off to your parents' house at this moment. By all means stay and spend that quality time with your wife and child, but don't go inviting every man and his dog over to spend time bonding with your baby.

During the first year, when DO you come over, and what do you do?

THE OPEN OFFER

QUICK QUIZ

You text the new mom to see if you can come over to help her with the baby during your lunch break. She texts you back to say thanks but tells you that everything is under control. You remember her social media post with a comment about how little time she now has after having a child. You're quite sure that she could use a couple of child-free hours. What do you do?

A. Clearly the overwhelmed new mother is frazzled and needs a rest yet she is too proud to ask for help. Show up at her house anyway and take care of the child for an hour over your lunch break. You'd love to see the baby!

B. Again, let her know that if she needs help at any time, you will be happy to babysit. In the meantime, go about your day as usual.

C. Pop over to her house for a coffee with toys for the child to stay entertained and food for the mom so that she doesn't need to cook. What are friends for, right?

D. Give her a call and ask if she is doing okay.

Well this one is tricky because it depends on what your relationship is like with the child's mother. Are you a good friend, an acquaintance, or a relative where real "friendship" is not necessarily the foundation of your relationship?

If you were really good friends, any one of the answers above would be acceptable. But if you *were* really good friends and she did need help, chances are that if she hadn't already been sending out SOS calls in your direction, she would have accepted your offer for help without hesitation.

The safest answer if you're unsure of how to define the closeness of your relationship is (B). Leave an open offer. This way she knows that you are genuinely there to give her a hand when she needs it, and not just there to see the baby. Don't insist on popping over. Sometimes mothers need space, or if they're trying to put their children into a routine, your visit can disturb that process.

CLARISSA SHARES: "My sister-in-law used to call me to say she would be over for coffee to have a chat and catch up. I thought it was nice considering we had not had that type of relationship before. But when I would tell her that the baby would be napping, she would just reply with something like 'Okay, then I'll pop over another day when the baby's awake.'

"On days when she would come over she would often just greet my child and head straight over to playing with her, shooing me off to 'take a break.' I felt she was there more for my child than to check in with me. I started to resent her visits because they were always guised as a way of 'helping' me when I didn't request or need it. If I had a few spare minutes to entertain her visit, then I would have preferred to spend those with my baby, considering *she* would just be over to play with the baby anyway."

FEEDING THE BABY

There are some things that you simply don't do with a baby that is not your own. It doesn't matter how close you think you are to the parents. A baby is a little person. He or she is not an extension of you no matter how similar they may look like their parents, or even yourself if you're a relative.

A Quick List of What Not to Do

- Don't feed the baby half-bitten food where you or somebody else has bitten the other half. Utensils always. Why? Babies don't need germs, or worse, incurable viruses like herpes. They don't even need to start adopting bad habits like sharing half-eaten food with people. This one is quite logical. But the parents do it? They're his *parents*. Not his uncle, aunt, grandma, grandpa, grandma's friend . . . you get the picture.
- Don't feed the baby by sticking your fingers in their mouth.
- Don't stick your fingers in the baby's mouth!

- Don't squish food with your fingers and then feed it to the baby. Baby eating utensils exist for a reason. Don't feed the baby in a manner in which you would not feed yourself.
- For goodness sake, don't chew food and then feed it to the baby.

The general rule is don't do something you wouldn't want to see the baby repeat. Because that's what they do. They watch and then they imitate.

A mother once told me that her eight-month-old daughter was always given blueberries to eat for breakfast, and she ate them herself every day without any problems. One day her overbearing sister-in-law came over and upon seeing this, insisted that the blueberries were too big, so proceeded to squash the blueberries between her fingers before putting the blueberries in the baby's mouth—all this despite the fact that the mother had told her to let the baby eat for herself. The following day, instead of eating the blueberries, the mother found squished blueberries all over the highchair. And this continued for months.

What is wrong with this? It's just a couple of squashed blueberries, right? Wrong.

What's wrong is that the sister-in-law completely ignored what the mother had instructed with regards to how to take care of her baby. And then she carried out the task at hand in a woefully hopeless manner. Using a knife to cut the fruit would have been a better option considering that's what adults do. Then leaving the fruit on the plate for the baby to eat, as usual, would have been the way to go instead of sticking her fingers in the baby's mouth.

Of the million and one things that mothers need to take care of, adding an extra task where there wasn't one before is just not cool.

Here are a few notes regarding food at specific ages, some of which we would be forgiven for not knowing, seeing as often the information isn't publicized enough to be part of our everyday common knowledge. Nevertheless, they are important and should be remembered.

Honey (For Infants Under 12 Months)

For someone who is not a parent, it seems odd that honey is a no-go zone for babies under one year old. After all, honey is natural. And natural things surely can't be harmful. But they can. In the case of honey, it's potentially lethal for a baby because there is a risk that it could cause botulism. And that is some serious shit. Artisan honey carries an even higher risk. So just keep that in mind. Honey is not a "better" substitute for sugar for infants under twelve months.

A Note on Candy (For Infants)

Today it is clear that sugar is not good for us, especially for young children. Many parents say that eating foods containing refined sugars cause their children to become hyperactive and difficult. But research mainly shows that sugar is not good for a child's teeth, even if they are just budding, and that early exposure to sugary foods can lead to sweet taste preferences when the infants become toddlers.[9] It goes hand in hand with don't feed the infant anything the parents don't want you to feed him or her, but more explicitly don't bring the infant candy and then ask the parent in front of the child whether or not they can eat it. Putting mom or dad in the bad guy position here is not very considerate at all. If you want to give the child candy or junk food, always check with one of the parents *first* to see if it's okay to offer it to the child, while the child isn't there. And don't say, "It's just a little bit" if the parent says no.

---

[9]Devenish, G., Mukhtar, A., Begley, A., Spencer, A. J., Thomson, W. M., Ha, D., Do, L., & Scott, J. A. (2020). Early childhood feeding practices and dental caries among Australian preschoolers. *The American journal of clinical nutrition*, nqaa012. Advance online publication.
[https://doi.org/10.1093/ajcn/nqaa012]

Soft Drinks for Infants and Toddlers

There is enough information out there now to let us know that soft drinks have zero nutritional value and are not good for health. No, cola in its form today was not invented by a doctor and therefore accepted as remedial or okay to give to infants or toddlers. Cola contains caffeine, which should not be given to children, especially infants or toddlers. It also is acidic, which can erode tooth enamel. And it's high in sugar, which can cause cavities even in teeth that have not yet sprouted. So if you're taking care of a baby that is not your own, not even a sip of cola for a baby or infant to "taste" is a good idea. A baby will likely drink anything they are given. It's your responsibility as the adult to make the right judgment calls on what you will put in front of them.

Salt for Infants and Toddlers

Infants who are breastfed or still drinking formula are consuming the right amount of salt for their age. When they start on solids, you might taste their food and think it's too bland and boring, so the temptation to add salt is huge. However, consider this. These are the guidelines to how much salt a baby and infant needs. A baby up to twelve months should have less than 1g of salt (that's 0.4g of sodium) per day. At one to two years old, they can have up to 2g of salt per day. That's about one-third of a teaspoon over an entire day. This is because they're infants. Their kidneys can't handle more than that. Too much salt in a baby or even a child's diet can have very serious consequences, including salt poisoning that can lead to permanent damage to the body's organs, coma, or even death. Make sure that you don't feed the child readymade food for adults because often they're high in salt. If you're preparing food, then don't add salt. Young children don't need it!

Cow's Milk for the Baby

A baby should not switch to drinking pasteurized cow's milk instead of breast milk or formula until after they are one year old. Contrary to some traditional beliefs, formula is not more "fattening" or "bloating" than cow's milk. In fact, cow's milk is concentrated in proteins and minerals that a baby cannot digest. This causes stress to their kidneys, which can result in severe illnesses. What about fresh cow's milk from a farm? That's possibly worse. Think about it, cow's milk is what a growing calf drinks. How big are they compared to a human baby?

Cow's milk also doesn't have the necessary nutrients a baby needs whereas formula and breast milk does. Formula is based on the elements of breast milk. It's an alternative to breast milk because it attempts to mimic the nutrients in breast milk, not regular cow's milk that we drink as adults.

Tea for the Baby

Teas are not good for babies because they contain tannins. Tannin is not the same as caffeine. You can have teas without caffeine that still contain tannin. Tannins have been shown to adversely affect the absorption of iron in our bodies. Growing babies need iron in their diets and this is something that is found in breast milk and formula. A lack of iron can lead to a myriad of developmental problems.

DISCIPLINING THE CHILD

A big mistake that a lot of people without children unknowingly make is that they intervene when a parent is disciplining their child. When a mother or father says no, and then the child looks to you for the same thing, the answer from you should also be no. Looking at the mother and asking, "Can I?" after you've seen what has just happened is not the right thing to do. Comments in front of the child, including "Aww poor thing, cake is *so* delicious. Are you sure she can't have sugar, not even just a bit?" is just as bad. Speaking to the child and saying something like "No, your mom won't let me give you the cake. Yes, Mommy's very cruel," is a huge no-no. Never force the parent into the role of the "bad" guy, just so you can then be the "cool aunt," "nice grandma," or "favorite uncle." A parent usually says no because they want what is best for the child, including teaching them discipline, delayed gratification, or simply because they don't want them to have refined sugar. Young children learn quickly. When rules appear "flexible" because Mom doesn't allow this, but Grandma does, then the rule doesn't exist in their world.

Disciplining children can be a very sensitive topic. At the risk of copping flak, *I* believe that you just don't hit a child. Nothing good comes of it. You want them to remember that they were spanked when they did something bad. But will they remember that connection? They won't understand *why* it was wrong, just that you hit them.

However you decide to discipline your child, physically disciplining a child that is not your own is a HUGE NO. You don't touch a child that is not your own, even if your intentions are good—even if you're from a different generation and that's what you did, and look how well your kids turned out. No. These are NOT your kids. Unless your title is Mom or Dad, you are not entitled in any way, shape, or form to physically discipline a child. Even then, if you were Mom or Dad, I would highly recommend steering clear of physical discipline—especially at the child's young age because you are where your child goes for safety. It's a total misfiring in their brains when their point of safety physically hurts them. There is plenty of research that shows a link between physical discipline and aggression, poorer brain development, and plenty of other issues . . . and very little to show that corporal punishment works in disciplining children.[10]

Also, please don't give advice on disciplining children that are not your own. "In my day we spanked a child when they did that." Or "You should never say the word 'no' to a child." It's one thing to throw into conversation the latest child discipline methods, but it is an annoying other to advise on it in the imperative like a professional.

Unfortunately, it may happen that you are witness to a parent going too far in disciplining their child and creating a frightening and possibly unsafe environment. If this is the case, and there is nobody else that will do it, then you need to step in. There are moments when many parents feel rage toward their children. Maybe an irritable child throwing their lunch on the floor is the proverbial straw that breaks the camel's back. However, at this stage, a child's safety and well-being is completely in the hands of the

---

[10] Gershoff, E. T., Goodman, G. S., Miller-Perrin, C. L., Holden, G. W., Jackson, Y., & Kazdin, A. E. (2018). The strength of the causal evidence against physical punishment of children and its implications for parents, psychologists, and policymakers. *The American psychologist,* 73(5), 626–638.

Tomoda, A., Suzuki, H., Rabi, K., Sheu, Y. S., Polcari, A., & Teicher, M. H. (2009). Reduced prefrontal cortical gray matter volume in young adults exposed to harsh corporal punishment. *NeuroImage*, 47 Suppl 2(Suppl 2), T66–T71.

parents. And if the parents cannot control their temper to a level that is on the right side of outright abusive, then they need therapy. If you're the only one to bring this up, then unfortunately you've drawn the short straw. At that critical moment you need to either find a way to diffuse the situation or remove the child from the situation. Tread lightly, but just going in to ask if there is anything you can help with or suggesting a *specific* thing with which you can assist, can help the parent check themselves. Oftentimes it's a feeling of guilt, tiredness, being overwhelmed or a mix of these that can cause a parent to lash out at their children. It's not fair, but it's human. Do your best not to judge them. Instead, try to help them.

BABYSITTING

If you're taking care of the baby, try to follow what the baby's mother has given you as a guideline. She knows her child best.

Wearing Out the Baby So That They Will Sleep Better Later

There is an old theory that children sleep better when they don't sleep during the day and are tired out from play. Unfortunately, this is not true. Young children don't function like adults because they get "over-stimulated," which means that it can take them a long time to calm down and settle to sleep.

When you are taking care of somebody's child, ask what are the baby's sleep cues. What should you be watching for as an indication to put them down for a nap? If you see that the child is clearly sleepy, put them down for a nap. If their parents have given you an indication of what time the child usually naps, try to wind down the activities to slower, quieter ones such as reading about half an hour before trying to put them down to sleep. There are many well-meaning caregivers who try to keep children awake, so that when they return to their parents it's "time for bed." However, more often than not, this results in the child possibly sleeping for a short while before waking up soon after instead of sleeping through the night—the result of over-stimulation.

Playtime with Children

It's difficult for someone who isn't a parent to understand how appreciated positive and almost cheesy sounds, songs, toys, or children's expressions can be to a parent. When babies are young and learning, their world is full of wonderment. The toys and songs aimed at children these days try to create that interest. Think about it. You won't hear a baby's toy say in a dull voice, "Yeah, yeah, this circle is green." Or let out an exasperated "Hi . . . oh it's you again." Instead you hear upbeat, chirpy voices sing-songing what we already see as fact.

"Green! The circle is green!" And *"Hello! Nice to see you again!"*

It may be tempting to laugh or scoff at the enthusiastic cheesiness of these games or toys. You may feel uncomfortable singing along with the songs, which of course you're not forced to. Just try to refrain from rolling your eyes, laughing mockingly at the toys, songs, or excited child, or in any way scoffing, even to other adults around. Children sense and comprehend the unspoken gestures, behaviors, or expressions. Go along with the child's excitement and energy. To them, everything is still new. You want to make it a joy for them to discover every little thing from shapes to numbers, colors to music.

Phones, iPads, and Screen Time for Children

Research has shown that no amount of TV for children under two years old is beneficial to their development. In fact the World Health Organization would like to see that children under two years old are not given any screen time at all. But let's not get too crazy here. The rationale is that children should be playing and encouraged to engage in physical activity. However, one more disturbing issue about children and screen time is the potential effect that our latest gadgets with screens can have on children's eyes. There isn't conclusive evidence yet in humans, but research has shown in animal studies that blue light (emitted from LED-lit screens such as flat screen TVs, iPads, smartphones etc.) can cause permanent damage to the retina at the back of the eye.[11] On top of that, we know that more blue light reaches a child's retina than an adult's. And we know that a damaged retina can lead to all kinds of visual impairments, including blindness.

When babysitting, try to use these devices as little as possible. There are plenty of activities you can do with a child without resorting to putting them in front of a screen. Singing, dancing, doing things that may seem repetitive to us adults can be enjoyable for a baby such as peek-a-boo, rolling a ball or shaking a bottle with something in it. For small babies, you don't even need to change activities often. If you see the baby looking away, often it's not because he's bored, it's because he's attempting to not become over-stimulated. Either that, or he's tired. If you're pottering around the house, give the child something safe to play with. Talk to the child, even if they don't yet "understand," and know that the interaction you are having with the child is already much better than the passive engagement of watching TV.

---

[11] Geiger P., Barben M., Grimm C., Samardzija M. (2015) Blue light-induced retinal lesions, intraretinal vascular leakage and edema formation in the all-cone mouse retina. Cell Death Dis. 2015 Nov 19;6:e1985. doi: 10.1038/cddis.2015.333.

Creating New Rules, Habits, or Routines That Go Against Those the Parent Is Trying to Establish

It's not always easy to give toddlers the sense of rules or routines. A lot of teaching good habits is derived from a continuous routine. Often this means that parents trying to establish rules or routines have gone to some effort in doing so—be it sacrificing outings, taking the time and effort to teach a baby to feed themselves (in the beginning it's almost always less messy to feed the baby spoon to mouth than to let them practice autonomy), teaching them to pack their toys away, or encouraging them to self-settle for bed. Whatever those rules or routines are, try your best not to break them while you're looking after the child.

It can be difficult when you're not used to the way the child's parents do things. For example, you may want to hold the baby and settle him to sleep in your arms each time he goes down for a nap, but you don't want the child to become dependent on that if he had a different sleep routine before. A full-time parent probably doesn't have the time to settle a toddler to sleep like that multiple times a day. Try to be extra considerate about these types of matters.

BE AWARE OF YOUR OWN BEHAVIOR

A baby comes into the world not knowing these things:

1. Social norms of engagement
2. Stereotypes and discrimination
3. Sarcasm/Joking

Babies and toddlers are processing things as reality. Despite their sometimes seemingly witty responses or curious whys, they're not yet able to analyze and critically assess what they are being told. If you tell them things like "boys don't cry," they will believe that. Their minds are absorbing information that will likely form their subconscious later in life. It's no wonder why so many fallacies continue to be believed, like "If you get cold, you will catch a cold," and why we find it so hard to shake these phrases from our own use even when we know them to be untrue! It's important not to make these types of statements to young children, even if they seem not yet to understand. Babies actually understand a lot more than we imagine. Many times it *seems* like it happens overnight—that they suddenly "understand" your phrases and directions—but they've been absorbing and impressionable for a while.

Comments that encourage discrimination toward others, even in a joking manner, cannot be made lightly in front of children. For example, "Ew, don't learn French because French people are all snobs." Or "We can't trust him because he's Italian and Italians are all criminals." These are all things that will build their subconscious. And in the end, who does discrimination disadvantage most? The person who is discriminating. It turns them into a closed-minded bigot, unable to see the humanity in other people just because of their race, color of their skin, sports team they support etc. This will hinder their ability to develop empathy. In short, babies don't need to adopt politically incorrect views or antisocial behavior.

WHITNEY RECOUNTS, "My husband's well-and-truly adult age sister would always make antisocial comments to my child to reveal all the negative thoughts going on in her mind. She'd say things like 'Good job not smiling to those idiots. Daddy's friends are idiots.' Or gesture 'He's crazy' when complete strangers complimented my daughter. She would teach her things like 'Flip the bird at those losers walking on the street!' while we were in the car and laugh like it was some type of anti-institutional hurrah.

"Even though this type of behavior comes naturally to my sister-in-law, and I know she doesn't mean any malice, I made sure to limit my daughter's exposure to her. I don't want to build that type of attitude into my daughter's subconscious as 'normal.' I could totally see why my sister-in-law was living a lonely, unfulfilled life. It was clear that she had a deeply ingrained superiority complex."

In this case, the mom did well because it's almost impossible to change an adult if that is the type of behavior that allowed them to progress into adulthood. Even if she were to approach her sister-in-law directly regarding these specific situations, her sister-in-law's character will seep through in other ways that will affect the child if she were to spend more time with her.

A Baby Is Not Your Emotional Dumping Ground

Some people have pets with whom they talk to throughout the day. In baby-voice, almost anything can seem acceptable when spoken out loud. It makes all your irrational or sometimes negative thoughts seem somewhat more bearable. You vent; you mutter. You're basically talking to yourself but with an audience so that makes you feel a little more "heard."

A pet will never refute anything you say. They're the silent audience.

A baby makes the situation seem even less crazy because you're not talking with an animal but with another human being. Tiny as they may be, in your mind there is the slightest possibility that they will comprehend what you're saying, so you continue with your commentary on that terrible date you went on, how all men are bastards, how your mother ruined your life, how your friends are all doomed, how climate change is the fault of us terrible humans, how the world is falling into disrepair—all while taking care of the child, and maybe all in a cute baby voice. It may sound crazy, but believe it or not, some people will actually do this. If this is you, please don't. A child is a child for a short time in their lives. They may not comprehend completely what you are saying but as their minds are sponges at this stage, it can't possibly help to have this negativity around.

Leave the emotional baggage for the adults in your life or your therapist. Try to remain positive around children.

VACCINATIONS

It's understandable that some people may not like the idea of vaccinating their babies. The pain they'll be in while getting the shots, the scars that might remain after some vaccinations, the voluntary injection of *diseases* in perfectly healthy young bodies. I get it. I'm a mother too. But personally I was much more at ease with taking my child outdoors or letting others hold her after she had some of her shots.

A first time mother may build up the first vaccination in her head as though it deserved the drama of a surgical procedure. They can't understand the nonchalance in which a seasoned mom may respond upon hearing the news that their child is going in for a *vaccination*. But that's because it's not a big deal. When babies are due for their first vaccinations, often they cry for about ten seconds or less and then it's all over. In Italy, the nurses administering vaccinations command "*coccole, coccole,*" literally "cuddles, cuddles," to the guardian bringing the child in for the shots, immediately after. There's no time for slipping the baby's leg back into her onesie; that can be dealt with after she's soothed. And that's a great tip that's comforting for both baby and caretaker.

If you're not the parent of the child, you are in no place to push an anti-vaccination agenda onto the parents. Risking that child's life is not within your rights. There are strict laws and obligations regarding vaccination in many developed nations. For example, unvaccinated children may not attend pre-school and many daycare centers. These regulations are in place not only to protect the general masses of children, but to protect the child in case he/she has parents who are against vaccinations. But at the end of the day, vaccinating a child is the parents' choice.

Fortunately vaccinations are obligatory in most developed nations. But I'm going to bring this to your attention again here, just in case you haven't read up on what it means to vaccinate a child and what the implications are for not doing so. In simply understanding how a vaccination works, it usually stops one from hopping onto the anti-vax bandwagon, constructed by big pharma conspiracy theorists, or those who assume their basic knowledge of how things work is going to be superior to that of teams of scientists and medical experts who have researched and developed vaccinations for humankind their entire careers. It would take a very foolish (not to mention arrogant) person to assume that their "knowledge" on something is going to be better than an expert's when it comes to matters as widely rolled out, audited, and endorsed by medical, governmental, and health bodies around the world.

Say you're a DIY home renovations master. we're talking *truly* impressive. Would you trust yourself to design a bridge over the harbor you cross each day to go to work? Hopefully your answer was no. Because that would be an architect and an engineer's job. You would trust that they know their shit, the governing bodies would have inspected it, and it would be safe for you to use. Just like vaccinations are for *your* child to live disease-free. A homeopathic concoction is just not really going to cut it.

A vaccination is a small amount of the disease-causing bacteria or virus, administered in a controlled manner, according to a researched timing schedule. It goes into the child's body where the child's immune system is then triggered to build antibodies against the disease. Without this, how else is a child to build these antibodies? Uncontrolled exposure to the bacteria/virus means catching the disease. If you think that is okay and that "natural immunity" is better, just Google Image "whooping cough infant" or "measles infant." Would you want to see your baby, a friend's baby, your grandchild, or niece/nephew suffer through this? Apart from what physically looks painful, many preventable diseases can cause permanent brain damage, autism, and central nervous system damage, not to mention death in young children. Where preventable, this should just never be a risk worth voluntarily taking. The risk associated with those diseases is higher than the risk of a severe adverse reaction to a vaccine. There needs to be a healthy respect for the scientists who spend their lives in this field of work.

An argument a lot of people who are against vaccinations use is that these diseases are already eradicated in our country, so why do our babies need to be vaccinated? The reason is simple. Globalization means that people travel frequently. With people, diseases travel too. To be termed "eradicated" just means that for one year there are no reported cases of a disease. But that's just *reported*. When the disease still exists in the world, it is possible that due to travel there may be outbreaks of the disease, such as measles in the USA in 2019—a disease once thought to have been "eradicated" in the USA.

Another argument is that if every child should be vaccinated so that we can protect all children including those not vaccinated, why can't our child be one of those who are not vaccinated? The reason is because there are legitimately those who cannot get vaccinated, who would be in a compromised position to fight the possible diseases they could be infected with. For example, children who are too young cannot be vaccinated, children who have had transplants and are on immunosuppressant medications can't get vaccinated. Children undergoing cancer treatment cannot be vaccinated, yet these children would be high risk if they were to contract any one of the diseases vaccinations can prevent. No one wants a tiny newborn to catch measles in their first months of life because of exposure to unvaccinated children. Some would say that the parents of those unvaccinated children are not only uninformed, but selfishly so.

Finally, another popular argument is that vaccinations cause autism. The reason this is out there is no thanks to a doctor who was stripped of his medical license due to this fraudulent claim. It turns out he was also being funded by attorneys who were seeking to file lawsuits against companies manufacturing vaccines. Interestingly enough, what *did* cause many cases of autism in the US in the 1960s was rubella—a disease now preventable thanks to vaccines. There is just overwhelming evidence that vaccines are safe and don't cause autism. And it's important to keep in mind that the risks of severe adverse reactions to vaccines are heavily outweighed by those associated with these preventable diseases.

If parents are sitting on the fence or really hating the idea of bringing their child in for vaccinations, just inform them of how a vaccination works and what the alternatives were to be if the child were not to be vaccinated. Google Images help a lot here. Hopefully you will be able to sway them into not running the risk.

MOTHER KNOWS BEST

There is a reason why pediatricians always tell mothers to make a visit to the doctor if they notice something "off" about their child. Pediatricians who spend their entire days with children, who've studied and built careers on children's health will tell you that a mother's intuition is always valid and shouldn't be ignored. So when the baby's mother is worried about something regarding her baby, don't shoo her concerns away. A mother's intuition here refers to a mother's "gut feeling" regarding her child, not her instinct to suddenly be nurturing, selfless, and a full-time caregiver. The jury's still out on that one.

Whether you believe that maternal "instinct" is real in terms of biochemical science or not, it can be argued that somehow mothers are often the most in-tune with their babies. Almost every mother can tell you of at least one incident that supports this theory. Ever wonder why a mother can often translate what their baby is trying to convey when all we hear is babble? It could well be that the mother is often the one who spends the most time with the baby. During that time she is responding to the baby's needs constantly and this is all a form of learning about her child in a way that is not necessarily intentional. When she has a gut feeling about something regarding her child, usually she draws from her experiences and what she knows of the world and of her child and is able to realize when something is off, or what the child may be experiencing.

CHRISTINE'S THREE-YEAR-OLD BOY went missing during a barbecue lunch at her house where her family was entertaining guests. She knew intuitively that he must have gone up into the mountains behind their home. Her reasoning was that he seemed fascinated with the butter knife he had been given during lunch. She reasoned that he must have imagined he could go up the mountains to slay the "wolf" that they always warned him would come down to eat him whenever he told a lie. While various members of the family went into the town, to the police station, to the neighbors' houses, Christine walked up the mountain. Low and behold, she found her son there, having been taken in by an old woman who saw a little boy with a butter knife walking alone in the mountains.

On exactly my daughter's first birthday, we were staying at a hotel and she had to take antibiotics for a nasty infection caused by a spider bite on her leg. I put her in her bed as usual and went to sleep. I was fast asleep when I suddenly felt *something* was wrong. I sat up in bed, turned on the lights and looked over at my daughter. Less than ten seconds later, she started to vomit *a lot*. She didn't wake from her sleep until I picked her up so I can't imagine what might have happened had I not been awake.

BABY'S BIRTHDAY

There is one big rule that lasts over the child's entire childhood years and that is not making plans for the baby on his birthday unless you are his parents. Don't even "run it by" the parents first. The parents will arrange for this if they wish to. And especially don't plan to spend a child's birthday without their parents. You may think of it as a sweet gesture. Just a special day for the baby and his grandparents, godparents, or his favorite aunt or uncle! But this is totally overstepping the boundaries.

Another thing to be cautious of, especially when the baby is a bit older, is not to buy big gifts for the child that you know his parents had in mind and thereby stealing their thunder. That's usually not appreciated and for a lot of people considered overcrossing boundaries too. Usually your intentions are only good and you just want what you believe the child would enjoy the most, however if you know that that is what the parents' wanted to buy the child because the child has been requesting it, you swooping in to buy the gift first is just not nice at all.

If you want to go ahead and spend big on the child's present, just be aware of the situation first. You might want to give the child everything you couldn't have or that you couldn't give your own child. It comes from such a good place but can be misaligned with what values his parents are trying to teach him. This is especially the case if they too have the means to purchase those big-ticket items but have chosen not to do so. If this is not the case, and the parents genuinely cannot afford the big-ticket items but would sorely desire them for their children, then it could be a great gift for the parents and the child to receive, as long as the intention isn't for them to then feel indebted to you.

First-Year Advice Geared to Husbands

The first year can be a tricky time, but by the end of it you will get the hang of being a father. After the first few months, you may start feeling like you have more of a bond with your child. If you've been actively involved in taking care of the child in the first few months, then it does get easier.

Your Relationship With Your Wife

An important thing that parents need to remember (often it's the mothers more so than fathers) is that even though there is now a child, your partner still needs to be the one that comes first. It's important that you see your wife not only as a mother now, but firstly as your partner. After having a child, taking care of the child, and possibly finding it difficult to get back into pre-baby shape with pre-baby energy and pre-baby sleep, your wife is probably finding it difficult to feel like an attractive woman again. More likely she feels like an exhausted, happy-to-make-it-out-of-the-house-with-clean-clothes mother. Or like someone who needs to now play a "motherly" role, the one painted by society as being the endlessly giving and sacrificing parent. This will get better with time. Eventually, you will both find that being the best version of yourself is the best way to parent and be a role model. However, it's never too early to start trying to make her feel attractive.

QUICK QUIZ

Your wife says in defeat, "I don't look good in any of my clothes anymore! My body won't bounce back." How would you respond?

A. Reply "Yeah but you've had a baby! You've created life and that's what is important. That makes your body special."

B. Say "Don't worry babe, I'll join a gym with you so we can both get fit again." And then pay for a gym membership.

C. Deny, deny, deny. Say "What do you mean? You look great to me!"

D. The sandwich method. Positive, negative, positive. "You still look great. What do you mean? At the most you probably just need a bit of toning, but your body created life. Cut yourself some slack."

Which reply did you choose?

The truth is that every woman wants to hear answer (C). Women are the harshest critics on themselves as is. They see fat where no one else in the world does. They see the imperfections that don't exist. When your wife who has had a baby in the past year makes a comment like this, it's not for you to jump in and save the day. Resist that. Nobody really wants a solution. She just wants to feel attractive again. If you chose answer (D), then you've not really saved the day by offering a solution or bettering the situation. You've foolishly mentioned toning where she hadn't mentioned it at all. Now you've given her something else to worry about. The general rule here is to just always try to make your wife feel attractive. You will come out better for it too.

Social Calendar

With a new baby in the family, there are a few adjustments to your lifestyle that you and your wife might need to make. If you're the first couple amongst your group of friends to have children, they may not understand what having a child really entails and this can make it more difficult for you to adjust without FOMO rearing its ugly head on occasion. Your friends may be planning a big night out at the club with tables and champagne showers, the works. For you it's either find a sitter and both you and your wife go, you go and leave your wife at home with the baby, your wife goes and leaves you with the baby, or you both pass up this sure-to-be epic night. What do you do?

There is no right or wrong answer here. What's your motivation for going to the club? Is it to dance because you like dancing? To soak in the atmosphere? To listen to loud music? To just let loose and forget that you're now an adult with the responsibility of raising another human being? God knows every parent needs one of those occasions every now and again. Again, there is no right or wrong answer. But generally, I truly believe that children are happier when their parents are happy and not a couple of angry, resentment-filled robots playing the role of a happy, "perfect" parent that general society seems to find acceptable. Just remember that it's not only *your* happiness that is important, but also that of your wife. Happy wife, happy life, right?

It cannot be said enough that your life *is* going to change after having a child. There may be people in your life telling you that nothing changes, that you can go about your life with the baby strapped onto you like a backpack and carry on as if you were pre-child, but that's just not true. Consideration must be given for the child as being a whole different human being with needs that must be fulfilled by an adult.

Once a child reaches about twelve months, provided that they don't have any developmental disorders, some kind of routine can usually be reached. Routine means when they sleep, when they eat, wash their hands, clean their teeth, have a bath etc. Make no mistake, reaching a place where you can call it a "routine" takes effort and sacrifice on the main caregivers' time, as well as support from those surrounding the child. If you are not one of the main caregivers to your child, your role is to support this process of arriving at a routine. If you come home late and your child is already getting ready for bed, don't expect to play and spend time with him that evening. If your parents want to pop over while the child is due for a nap, make sure that they know the child will be sleeping.

Just as we as adults need to know what's going on, children do as well. Imagine if you're relaxing on the couch, near-ready for bed. You've found something easy to watch on TV and wind down for the day. You're looking forward to having a bit of quiet time to shut off your brain . . . and then your wife suddenly pops in, fully dressed, and tells you that she has invited ten guests over for a late dinner. That would be annoying at best, but mostly quite stressful. Well, that's the life of a backpack baby. You know the one, the poor baby that's strapped into a BABYBJÖRN carrier and out and about all day and all night. With this stress it's no wonder that these parents just can't seem to get their children to sleep through the night.

Of course there will be days when you can't follow the child's routine. But it doesn't mean that you should give up on the idea completely because it "just doesn't suit your lifestyle." This is just the tip of the iceberg as to what parental sacrifice is about. Think of it this way—the quicker you're able to establish a routine for the child, the quicker you will be able to gauge how much time you have for yourself and your wife.

QUICK QUIZ

You and your wife have been invited to dinner with friends at a fancy restaurant in a week's time. It's a Michelin-star restaurant and you haven't seen these friends in months. Your baby has been fussy for the last few days, as she is teething and only wants her mother. Because of this she has fallen out of her sleeping routine and is now awake until 10 p.m. even though you've been trying to get that time back to 8 p.m. What do you do?

A. Accept the invitation because in a week's time your baby may be back to her normal self and a sitter would be able to take care of her without any problems.

B. Accept the invitation and leave your wife at home with the baby after discussing this with her.

C. Accept the invitation and bring the baby with you to dinner. She's not sleeping until 10 p.m. nowadays anyhow. She'll be alright.

D. Turn down the invitation because you won't be able to have a good time knowing that your wife is going to have to take care of the fussy baby herself.

Again, a baby is not like a bag that you just strap into a carrier and take out with you whenever you have to or want to go out. She's not supposed to follow your schedule. Babies need to sleep and when they are usually asleep at 8 p.m. then yes, to keep all parties happy, the answer is (D). You will have to skip that dinner out with friends if you don't have somebody home to stay with the baby.

That said, turning down all invitations to go out with friends is also not a solution because it can lead you to becoming detached from your support network. Real friendships are important to maintain and social interactions keep us connected to our community. The best you can do in this situation is to acknowledge that this teething phase is going to be temporary and there will be other occasions when both you and your wife will be out to social events together with friends again.

Expectations of Your Stay-At-Home Wife to Do Other Things outside of Taking Care of the Child

Saying that taking care of a child is a full-time job is inaccurate because it's not. It's much more demanding. It's like a full-time entrepreneurial role where you don't actually ever "switch off" or "clock out" of work. If your wife has given up her career or gone from full-time work to part-time to take care of your child, make no mistake that this *does not* mean that now she can also be your private secretary, doing your bitch work and keeping your schedule.

If you're with your child long enough on any given day, you will realize that "me" time somehow gets zapped away. There may be days when your child refuses to take his naps, days when he's sick, days when he's crying more than normal, days when he won't feed or days when you yourself are feeling out of sorts. On every one of these days, the primary caretaker needs to be switched on and able to deal with everything. So if that caretaker is your wife, cut her the slack that she most likely needs. When you get home, it's not now time for her to take care of you too.

She has spent the whole day caring for your child. If she's running a fever and you don't have other childcare options, she can't easily "call in sick" to this job. Seeing that she has those ten minutes or half an hour of rest while the child is finally taking a nap, don't assume that this is when she could "easily" do a round of laundry or run errands, or do this or that. No. She can't. A full-time mother needs downtime too. Unlike a fixed lunch break, these ten minutes here and there are all she's got to herself.

The job is ongoing with its perks as a parent, but it is also unpredictable and demanding. Even if your wife has decided to become a stay-at-home mom, don't immediately write off the idea of getting help either around the house or with the kids. It all depends what kind of lifestyle you are able to afford, who you want raising your child, and what type of expectations you have for your life after having a child. The key point is not to have expectations of your wife that are not realistic in this day and age. We are no longer in a world where women are expected to be completely selfless and sacrifice their *entire* lives and livelihoods for their families unless that is what gives them complete satisfaction.

QUICK QUIZ

Your wife works part time from home as a writer, so she chooses her own hours. You normally take care of the baby's bath routine after you've both cleared the dinner table. That's the time your wife normally uses to work. But there is a soccer match on TV that you want to watch tonight. What do you do?

A. Ask your wife to take care of the baby's nighttime routine. She can find extra time tomorrow to work.

B. Send the baby off to the grandparents' house. You can pick up the baby after the match, which finishes late by which time the baby will be fast asleep.

C. Luckily you arranged for the sitter to come in for a few hours to put the baby to bed. You anticipated this clash!

D. Begrudgingly take care of the baby and forego watching the soccer match.

What was your answer?

While it probably won't hurt to ask your wife every now and again if she can care for the baby during her couple hours normally dedicated to work, you shouldn't take for granted that just because she's working from home and selects her own hours, this time can be contaminated with other tasks, or completely hijacked. Respect the time that your wife has carved out for herself to work, work out, or just relax because—especially with work—new mothers usually have to learn to compartmentalize their time hard. This means that mentally, that precious hour or two that they've allocated, they've geared up for it. They're ready to go and ramp up fast. You taking that away at last minute's notice (or last day's notice) is inconsiderate. If you know your wife doesn't like the baby staying with the grandparents unattended, then don't choose that option. You know that your wife will have to give up her own time because doing so is her preferred option. Answers (C) or (D) are the only real choices.

A NOTE ON CAREGIVERS: OUTSOURCING VS. YOUR PARENTS OR HER PARENTS

Depending on where you live in the world, maternity leave, and sometimes also paternity leave, doesn't last forever. And not all mothers (or fathers) choose to go back to work after having a child. Whether the primary caregiver works or not, it should be well understood that parenting in itself is a full-time job. But *really* full time. There are no sick days, no fixed time coffee breaks or lunch hours, no time when you can "clock off" and just relax. In that first year, the primary caregiver to the child is basically on-call all the time, every day.

In the case where the primary caregiver is your wife and she might need a few hours to herself on occasion, you are posed with choices to make on who should take care of the baby while she takes a break from this job. Even if she is a superwoman, having somebody else take care of the child for just a few hours a week gives you time to spend together as a couple, which is very important for a healthy relationship, especially post-child.

If the grandparents live close, then this could be a win-win option that is usually very financially favorable too. However, many times couples choose not to go with a grandparent and instead elect to use a babysitter, a full-time nanny, or childcare center. To make the best choice, here are some variables you as a couple may consider:

- **Are the grandparents physically able to take care of the child to a level that won't put the child at unnecessary risk?**

  Babies and toddlers can be a lot of work. Keeping up with a toddler is tiring, especially if they are already running around. Young kids who need to be carried around can also be tiring. Out of sheer tiredness of bending up and down to place and pick up the child from the floor, I've heard of grandparents who rest babies on countertops for "just a second" while they turn around and answer the phone. The rest of the story doesn't need telling.

- **How long and how often do you need somebody else to take care of the child?**

Asking a grandparent to take care of a child for a couple of hours a week versus full time are two very different things. Depending on the child's age and personality you may prefer that he is in an environment with other kids, or one with specific activities selected to encourage his mental and physical development.

- **Whether or not you agree with the grandparents' approach to baby-sitting.**

Perhaps Grandma coos and goo-goo ga-gas to the child all day and you prefer she speaks with real words, or maybe she swears like a sailor. As much as you want to convince yourself that your child is just sporadically exclaiming and mispronouncing "fire truck", deep down you know that no mispronunciation has been made. Perhaps grandma's idea of baby-sitting is carrying on with her life while plopping an iPad in front of the child or feeding the child cola and candy. Or maybe Grandma is an old-fashioned type, drumming into your child outdated nonsense like "good girls don't run about and laugh so loudly." There are many reasons why leaving children with grandparents is falling out of favor. Usually these all lead back to a lack of respect for the parents being the parents and therefore the ones who determine how they would like their children to be taken care of. Grandparents are often not paid to take care of grandchildren, so it's seen as a "favor" when they do so. Applying stipulations such as "please don't give my child candy" therefore seems like a command to somebody already doing you a favor and that goes against what we are raised to find as a socially acceptable "transaction" if you will.

- **Whether you *and* your wife are on good terms with the grandparents.**

  Is there enough candor between you in which you can *both* openly discuss matters, or insist on a particular approach to raising or taking care of your child with the grandparents? For example, if the child's grandma wants to give the child a sip of soft drink and you don't want the child to touch the stuff, can you easily speak up? Will your requests be met or will they go in one ear and out the other?

It's not throwing your hands up in defeat when the necessity comes for hiring help to take care of your child. It may even be something positive that will enable you and your wife to reclaim a bit of your lives outside of parenthood, if not for just a few hours a week. Keep in mind that it's no one else's business to weigh in on this decision.

QUICK QUIZ

Under your care, your daughter has had an accident and been taken to the ER. Your wife is at work and won't be home until the evening. Meanwhile your wife's parents already know of the incident, as they live close-by, and have gone to the hospital with you. You are still at the hospital and they have told you not to call your wife and stress her out unnecessarily, as she will find out after work anyway. What do you do?

A. Call your wife and tell her what happened but assure her that she does not need to leave work early, everything is under control.

B. Call your wife and tell her she needs to leave work and join you at the ER in case they need information from the child's mother.

C. Don't tell your wife and wait until she arrives home from work.

Don't tell your wife at all. Hopefully you'll be out of the hospital and back home in time for dinner and she'll be none the wiser.

This is an incident that happened to yours truly. I got hit with a double whammy because while I was reluctantly heeding the advice from my in-laws of not telling my husband what had happened, his sister, who had found out from her parents, ran to tell him instead. Zero points for me in terms of taking care of our child, and zero also for marital trust.

It cannot be stressed enough how important communication is between a couple when they have a child together. Information regarding the child should *always* be shared between the couple first. This is paramount. If something were to happen to your child, such as an incident that would see one of you taking them to the emergency room, then the other parent should be contacted and filled in on the situation by their spouse. Whether or not the timing is right, as a parent, if you're on the receiving end of this information, you need to be able to deal with your emotions as an adult and continue to do what you need to do despite it. This is part and parcel with being not just a parent but an adult. If the situation is reversed, you need to also expect that your partner will be able to take the information, and respect them enough to give them the information in full. This is what "parenting together" is all about. So the answer here is (A). You give your wife the news. If you're really wonderful, you will also try and contain your emotions so that she can decide what she should do after receiving your information sans exaggerated hysterics (which, don't worry, seem to be the norm with a first born).

BE A REAL PARTNER

Many men who work still think that raising the child and keeping the house in order is the wife's job, regardless of whether or not the wife also holds down a paying job. If your wife has a paying job of any sort (it doesn't matter if she's part time or full time), then there is really no excuse for you to not be equals in the home as well. If she doesn't have a job, there needs to be a clear understanding that taking care of the child all day is not only physically tiring, but mentally demanding too. There is research that shows that a man's cortisol level will decrease if he comes home from work *and* his wife is busy working around the house.[12] It's not enough for a man to just come home and chill on the couch, his wife needs to be kept busy! It's no wonder that many women prefer their husbands at work rather than home breaking their balls.

As a husband, you must realize that the baby is yours together. This means that chores around the house and the baby need to be split fairly. There is what works best for you, and what works best for your wife, but then there is also what works best for the marriage. The marriage is a separate entity in itself that needs to be taken care of. Think of it this way. While you've been at work, so has your wife. So when you come home, *that* work at home needs to be split amongst you both. Don't go to her to ask for instructions or directions. Own that responsibility as your own. Don't, I mean really *DO NOT* say things like "I put the laundry in the washer for you," "I helped you unload the dishwasher," or "Do you want me to *help* you change the baby's diaper?" *Just do it!* It's as much your work as it is hers. Do it and shut up about it. Your wife will appreciate you all the more for it. And don't worry, in the 2020s your efforts will not

---

[12] Saxbe, D. E., Repetti, R. L., & Graesch, A. P. (2011). Time spent in housework and leisure: links with parents' physiological recovery from work. *Journal of family psychology : JFP : journal of the Division of Family Psychology of the American Psychological Association (Division 43)*, 25(2), 271–281.

go unnoticed (unlike a woman's effort in the domestic domain unfortunately).

TAKE PHOTOS

My final big tip is to take tons of photos and videos of your wife with the baby. They don't need to be perfect, your wife doesn't have to super presentable, you just need to have those pictures. Don't forget this because the year really will pass by quickly and mothers are often the ones taking the photos of baby with everyone *but* herself.

First-Year Advice for Those Close to the New Mom

For the Mother of the Mom AKA New Grandmother

During your daughter's first year of motherhood, she may often come to you for advice, help, or just someone to share her experience with. Your job is to actively listen and offer advice only if it's asked for. Parenthood may not look like what it looked like for you, but respect that decisions regarding the child should be made between your daughter and the child's father, whether they are married or not, provided he isn't some deadbeat.

Remember that it's always nice to offer some encouragement or words of praise where you see fit. There are mothers who raise their children the same way they were raised and there are mothers who raise their children differently because they saw room for improvement in their childhoods.

CRYSTAL SAYS, "Being a middle child, it always seemed like my mother didn't have time for me. My older sister was good at everything and my younger sister was the baby of the family. I often felt overlooked and unloved. I don't want that for my own children. I put my career on hold because I wanted to be able to give them the attention and love I knew I needed as a child."

However, like many mothers who choose to parent differently than their own mothers, Crystal has a good relationship with her mother. Her mother acknowledged how Crystal felt as a child and can understand why she chose her softer style of parenting. Crystal also acknowledged that her mother lived under different socio-economic circumstances, at a time where information on parenting was different, and was only a young mother herself. Just human after all, like herself today.

If you as the grandmother can take the first step in acknowledging that your daughter is doing a good job, possibly even praising her for finding solutions for where you fell short as a parent, you open the road to having a better relationship with your daughter post-child. If on the other hand, you cannot admit to yourself—let alone anybody else—that you did your best but were not aware that your child felt x, y or z, and therefore remain adamant that your daughter is now over-protective, over-caring, or just *extra*, then that puts you on the path of arriving at further resentment from your daughter as her child grows up. She may even limit the amount of time you spend with your grandchild.

If you feel the need to compliment *others* on how good they are with the baby (perhaps another one of your children, the baby's aunt or uncle), remember not to throw the baby's mom (or dad) under the bus just to make your compliment *especially* when it's done in front of the baby. We all get sensitive about people putting us down us in front of our own kids. Phrases like *"You're so much better with him than his own mom,"* or *"He prefers playing with you to his own father."* Even if it were true, neither of those comments is nice for a mother to hear. It's better to keep those observations to yourself, or try to pay a compliment without the comparison. Using the examples above would be to say something more like "Wow, *you're great with the baby,"* or *"The baby really loves to play with you."*

Genuine words of praise can be music to a new mother's ears. They're in a new role in their lives where they may second-guess everything they're doing. Hearing that they're doing a good job, be it similar to how you yourself parented or completely different, is reassuring. Offer this when you can and your daughter will likely have no problems referring to you positively to your grandchild even if she might be harboring any resentment over your style of parenting.

SISTERS AND BROTHERS

The first year of being a mother is a time of enormous transition and transformation for your sister. In the first few months (aka thrown in the deep end), she is forced to respond to everything the baby requires. While you might be over to see your cute niece or nephew for a few hours, she is living the reality of 24/7 caretaking of a baby. This is life-changing, and over the months as she becomes more accustomed to this new role, she may possibly suffer a bit of an identity crisis. You may also see her in a different light now too.

If you've always relied on your sister for help, emotional support, or time, you may find that now she has little time to offer. If you're very close, you may find it hard to understand how she can love this new human being so much and dedicate so much of her time to this baby. But give her time to adjust to this new lifestyle. There will come a stage when you realize that although motherhood has changed her, she is still essentially the same person.

Mothers of babies and young children are tired. That may as well be a fact. Your sister may have been able to stay up for late-night chats, or to go for that last-minute dash to the shops with you pre-baby. She may still really *want to*, but out of sheer exhaustion there is no more inviting option than getting some shuteye at every opportunity she can. She's not being a spoilsport and she's definitely not being lazy. She's a new mom. Only one who has had kids can fully understand what that means.

I remember constantly nagging my cousin to bring her super cute children over when they were young. I never realized just how much of a task that was until I became a mother. She lived in a different city, which meant that she had to catch a bullet train to arrive at our home (where there were plenty of more than willing people to babysit her kids). In hindsight, I realized that even packing for that travel would have to have taken a lot of organization, factoring in nap times and routines, let alone facing the daunting task of taking that trip with a two-year-old and a newborn. For how much I wanted them to come to visit, I really should have offered to take the train over to accompany them back.

The idea of luxury travel doesn't really exist for us normal folk. Even if your sister is flying business or first class with a baby, it's not all about kicking back, watching movies and sipping champagne. Unless your sister actually *has* a nanny traveling with her, she still needs to be doing nanny duties. The flight attendants are not going to be able to help her out in that department. Who will take care of the baby if she needs to use the bathroom? How do you handle a stroller and carry-on baggage in the airport? In transit? *With a baby?*

Depending on how close and capable you are, there are things you can do to help your sister out. Many times when you visit, you may think that taking care of the child is what your sister would like for you to do. But this is a misconception in many cases. If your sister doesn't have help in the house, it could be nicer for you to help pop in a load of laundry, help her out with things around the house, or bring over a meal so that instead of cooking she can have some quality time with her baby. It should go without saying that if you are having your sister and her baby over for a meal at your house, you should not let your sister be the one left on table clearing duties and loading the dishwasher while you sit and play with her baby. Her baby is her number one priority and your house is your responsibility. It really is as simple as that.

THIS ONE'S FOR THE PARENTS-IN-LAW

If your son and his wife choose to enlist the help of a babysitter or a daycare center despite your offers of assistance, don't be offended by this. There are a myriad of reasons why they may have chosen to go this route and there are few which involve them not trusting you to take good care of their child.

As much experience as you may have raising your own children, the world has changed a lot even in just the last ten years. This means that the typical family has changed. Nowadays Mom likely works as well as Dad. She may even work at a more demanding or higher salaried job. Now people work from home. There are jobs that exist that didn't in the past and there are former jobs that have gone away. This means that children need a different type of education in order to be equipped for today's more interconnected, more globalized society and culture.

What this also means is that "parenting," as seen in the traditional sense, may be different to what parenting entails today. You may see your daughter-in-law parenting in a completely different way to which you raised your children. Perhaps she drops off the young child at childcare in the morning and doesn't pick him up until the late afternoon. Perhaps she doesn't give him exactly what he wants when he starts crying. However much you may wish to give your opinion on what she's doing right or wrong, be careful not to rush to judgment. It may be helpful to point out the benefits of being on a school's parent-teacher-committee or of helping out at the child's playgroup or daycare center, but it should not be pressed upon with today's demands, especially on women who are still being led to believe that it is possible to be a superhero-type mother, wife, sister, daughter, daughter-in-law, career woman, and generally perfect. This is already an unfair, unattainable figment of some asshole's imagination and propagating that is not helpful for any woman.

One key idea to keep in mind is that all parents parent differently. There are those who believe that keeping the child alive is parenting and there are those who are gung-ho on giving their children a leg-up in the world from the very beginning. As long as the children are loved, kept healthy and safe, there is no "right" or "wrong" way to parent, there are just different ways.

BROTHERS AND SISTERS-IN-LAW

If you're from a tight-knit family where boundaries are often blurred, it may be difficult to distinguish where your opinion, advice, or help is welcome when it comes to your brother's child. You may have to hold your tongue at times but try to remember that there are many versions of parenting which are perfectly fine. They may not be what you see as "best," but they are nonetheless valid.

QUICK QUIZ

It's one of those occasions where the family is all together at somebody's house. But whose house? This is an important distinction. When it comes time to help around the house—be it preparing a meal, serving, or cleaning up after eating—who takes care of the baby if the occasion is at:

A. Your house.
B. Your parents' house.
C. A mutual friend's or any other relative's house.
D. The baby's mother's house.

How did you answer each of the questions above?

It's no big mystery that the mother is the one who takes care of the baby in every situation unless you're at the mother's house and she insists on doing the housework. In which case, you could always offer in any case.

In situations (A), (B), or (C), shirking away from housework to take care of the baby is simply not helpful and it's also kind of rude if the mother is then stuck with doing the cooking, cleaning, or whatever else it is. You may be *trying* to be helpful. After all, the "poor mother" has been "stuck" with the child the whole day or week or whatever. If this is the case, great! It's really lovely that you are thinking for her.

However, wouldn't it be nicer to help out with the cleanup, and *then* volunteer to take care of the child while you let the mother enjoy a peaceful coffee break or dessert after? That could align your actions with your intentions in a much better way!

Most parents are happy when those whom they love and trust love their children. They may actively involve you in the child's life because they see how much you enjoy spending time with the child and vice versa. As you try to solidify your identity in the child's mind as maybe the fun uncle or the cool aunt, keep conscious of the way you are doing it and the fact that after spending time with you, the parents will be the ones that have to go back to parenting. This means that if you paint Mom or Dad as the fun police, or if you give the child candy when you know their parents would hate that, you'll be sending them back to the parents after your play date. The parents will have to calm a child on a sugar high, be up at night to put a restless child to bed, and somehow explain why you have different rules to them. That is likely not going to end well for you.

Overstepping your boundaries and reprimanding your brother on how he is raising his child and then telling the child that his dad is an idiot is also not advised. Not only is it incredibly disrespectful to the child, your sister in-law, not to mention your brother, it doesn't show that you care more about the child than his own father. You're not going to be the "cool aunt." You're going to be the aunt to whom they limit their visits because she oversteps her boundaries.

FRIENDS OR RELATIVES WITH CHILDREN

Share Information!

Being a parent for the first time can be overwhelming. Today we have choices galore on just about everything and oftentimes it can be confusing, frustrating, and time-consuming to sort through all the information to arrive at the "best" solutions for our children. Being through this before, you can be a great resource of information, especially if you share a similar background (think values, socio-economic background, upbringing) to your friends going through parenthood for the first time.

Which car seat did you buy and why? What was your experience with it? What are the legal requirements? Which high chair did you go with? How did you decorate your nursery? Did you have to re-do it after a few short months? Which baby cot? Which nursery or daycare did you send your child to? Which pediatrician? How did you get your baby to sleep?

All of this can be helpful as long as you keep in mind a few simple rules:

1) Not all babies are the same. What worked for you may not work for this particular baby.
2) Not all parents have the same values or means as you.
3) Your choice is not the only choice.
4) Don't be snide if you never struggled with similar issues as this mother may be going through, even if your child was a perfect little angel in comparison to this nightmare baby.

You're sharing your experience, which is absolutely valid, but the fact that you've been through it before doesn't make you an expert on *someone else's* baby.

Remember how it was when you had your first child—the bombardment of advice, insistence, judgment, and downright criticism for your choices. Chances are that you are already quite careful of not doing the same. This is why friends and relatives with children (especially those with young children) can often be the best support group for a new mom.

When You Don't Share

If you are a parent and you don't want to share information or experiences with a struggling new mother, you might want to reflect upon why that is. Did you have a particularly bad experience with receiving too much unsolicited advice when you entered motherhood? Is the new mother the type that will shut down any advice that you give, or turn around and judge your approach to parenthood? Are you afraid that by giving hard-earned information on your end, you will disadvantage your own child because your friend's child may reap the benefits of your trial-and-error with your children?

If you have thought about why and decided that you prefer not to share, then this is also fair. It's not your obligation to do so. But it can be awkward when advice is explicitly requested. Identifying the root cause of this decision not to share can help you to check whether or not your reasoning is sound or a bit cuckoo. For example, if you did all the research on daycare centers to find the one your child went to, and your friend is asking if you have any recommendations and you say no because *you* did all the hard work finding this one. Your logic may be that their child will just skip along merrily to this ideal daycare without having to trial the others, whereas your child had to. But think about it this way, with or without your recommendation, your friend may stumble upon this daycare too. On the flip side, if you know the new mother to be the type to blame you should any of your recommendations not live up to her standards, then definitely, I wouldn't share either. Nobody needs to be on the receiving end of that type of behavior. Mothers are still human. They don't all suddenly become saints.

Listen and Validate Feelings

Whether you share information or not, you can help out a new mother just by listening and validating the emotions that they're feeling. Try not to 'shoo, shoo' them away as petty or to judge them (*how can you get mad when he is so adorable?*).

When You Parent Differently

People can be the best of friends, yet still choose very different parenting styles. Discussions about parenting can lead to all kinds of feelings from inadequacy that you're not doing enough, jealousy, incredulousness, even contempt. They're all very strong emotions because the subjects at hand are our children, and while children are so young and dependent on us we see them somewhat as the outcome of our parenting decisions.

At this stage of parenting, a parent is practically the sole decision maker of what this baby does - like the manager on a business project. Not all managers are going to supervise the same way, offer the same training, or even get the same outcomes. And many will rip apart the management techniques or philosophies of other managers, yet still enjoy a game of golf with them. The same can be said of parenthood and friendships. If you can't stand the way your friend is parenting or vice versa, don't bring it up in conversation. Spend some time together as friends without kids and agree to disagree. This can be easier said than done, especially if one of you are in the first few months of parenthood, but it's not altogether impossible.

FRIENDS OR RELATIVES WITHOUT CHILDREN

There's a very fine line to draw with close relatives without children, especially for those who have wanted children but were not able to have them for whatever reason. A baby in the extended family brings so much joy and there are times when you may feel, or those surrounding you such as your parents or your loved ones may feel, that this baby will somewhat "heal" the emotional wounds you've suffered from not having children of your own.

A friend once told me that her mother-in-law continuously repeated her own daughter's name to the baby, even going as far as to repeat "mama" to the new born while in her daughter's arms. This is not normal. And it takes away from the experience of a first-time mother, that of her first child calling her "mama" for the first time. This is really hurtful and in general just a dick move.

The same friend told me that her mother-in-law often made comments to the baby about how similar she was to her aunt (the mother-in-law's own daughter who did not have children). "She would say things like 'Yes, when you grow up, you will have curly hair too just like your Auntie Megan!' And that would get under my skin because it was just one of the many ways she tried to role play my daughter as her own daughter's baby."

So the fine line to draw is to realize that although you can shower the baby with love, keep in mind that if you still sorely want children of your own, don't accidentally take away from the experience of being a mother from the baby's actual mother.

That being said; thank God for friends without children! At a time when we have suddenly taken on this new responsibility and title of a 'mother,' we often begin to feel a bit old and 'out of the loop' when it comes to the latest trends, gadgets, music, beauty treatments, and basically everything not baby related. Here, friends without kids are invaluable to a new mom because spending time with you means we can indulge in being ourselves as individuals, as friends, and not just as moms.

When my first was a baby, I used to love catching up with my friends without children, listening to what they were up to. One was getting her book published, one had a flirtatious relationship in the office that *required* our dissection, another was planning a trip to South America with her fiancé, and another had chick-flick worthy stories about a European man she was seeing. Often being laughter-filled and so much fun, it was great to have my mind work in a different way again; to care about somebody and something else other than my child and whether or not I was doing enough kegels.

On the other hand, there isn't a problem with mothers who begin to only spend time with other mothers. I've covered why that might be so earlier in the book. If you've gone through the sections in here, thinking "that's not me, neither is that, nor that" to every possibility of how one might accidentally be getting on a new mom's nerves, don't be hurt by this because it's probably more out of necessity than design. Perhaps the new mom in your life has a lot of questions to ask, or a lot to rage about; which they feel would likely bore you. I don't have solid numbers but I would hazard a guess that it's very rare that a woman *completely* changes once she has a child. She's essentially still the same individual she was prior with the same interests, personality and character. Her priorities may change, but friendships usually survive especially if you're able to acknowledge that indeed she has had a child, what that really means for her day-to-day now, and that for at least a few years this is going to be the most precious thing in her life (meaning that even though she's allowed to say her baby's being an asshole today, you're not).

AFTERWORD

Being able to have a child is a blessing that brings with it an enormous sense of responsibility. They say it takes a village to raise a child, but often that village can make a new mother want to rip her hair out. Mothers are generally the ones to read the books and gather the information on pregnancy and the first year of a child's life yet a huge problem that many of them face is the onslaught of opinions, advice, comments, and insistence from those around them who feel they have a "stake" in the game.

In reading this, my hope is that you will be able to be part of this village in a positive way. You are somebody who cares about the well-being of either the mother or the child—hopefully both. Seeing that the well-being of the child often depends largely on the well-being of the mother, my hope is that you're now able to see how others' actions may affect her, and how you can help if that is your intention, or step back if it's not.

During the first pregnancy and the first year of raising a child, a mother can be pedantic and precious about her child. After all she is entering new territory as the primary subject. It's often said that with the first pregnancy a woman is all "no wine, no sugars, no coffee," and with their second they turn into "no limits." But that doesn't mean that either of the approaches are wrong or that one is better than the other. It's important to be sensitive in the first year. As the mother becomes more comfortable in this role and establishes a bond with her child, she will get over the preciousness to some degree and become more relaxed about letting you into her child's life.

In the meantime, remember to extend the open offer to help, and enjoy watching the child grow. If you are open to being in tune with others' responses and cues, you will find that a baby in the family, or amongst your close group of friends, can change not only their parents' lives, but your own life and perspective too.

ABOUT THE AUTHOR

Amy grew up in Sydney, Australia and currently lives in Milan, Italy.

Printed in Great Britain
by Amazon